FLANNERY O'CONNOR

GARLAND REFERENCE LIBRARY
OF THE HUMANITIES
(VOL. 221)

FLANNERY O'CONNOR
A Descriptive Bibliography

David Farmer

GARLAND PUBLISHING, INC. • NEW YORK & LONDON
1981

Library of Congress Cataloging in Publication Data

Farmer, David R.
  Flannery O'Connor, a descriptive bibliography.

  (Garland reference library of the humanities)
  Includes index.
  1. O'Connor, Flannery—Bibliography. I. Title.
II. Series.
Z8640.3.F38 [PS3565.C57]   016.813′54   80-8480
ISBN 0-8240-9493-X   AACR2

Printed on acid-free, 250-year-life paper
Manufactured in the United States of America

To N.K. and Patty Farmer
and to Laura Black;
and in loving memory of
Lydia B. Farmer, Laura J. Robb,
and Sarah Black

CONTENTS

ILLUSTRATIONS

ACKNOWLEDGMENTS

This bibliography could not have been completed without the assistance of a considerable number of people, many of whom have become good friends as the project moved forward. When I first began to assemble an O'Connor collection that would permit me to begin work on the bibliography, Franklin Gilliam and Anthony Newnham of the Brick Row Book Shop (then in Austin) would return from buying trips with needed periodicals and books in hand. In the later stages of my work, Hugh Chisholm in the Mirabeau B. Lamar Library, The University of Texas at Austin, gave valuable information on sources for translations, while Margie Cohn and Andreas Brown drew upon resources in New York to find materials. From London, Anthony Rota provided many of the English imprints. Finally, George Bixby turned up additional important and difficult-to-find works for description or verification.

As the project progressed, George Bixby offered cogent suggestions on format and organization and generously made available for study his extensive private collection. Indeed, he was the first person to give me information on the initial entry in Section B, *New Signatures I*. This elusive anthology contains a story by Flannery O'Connor which escaped previous bibliographical attention.

Also, I am grateful to Edwin Erbe for allowing me to examine several books from his private collection on occasions when I conducted research in New York. And for sound advice during the final preparation of my manuscript, I am indebted to Professor Joseph Katz, particularly for his helpful and careful suggestions on many bibliographical details and his recommendation to adopt the system of enumeration found in the "A" and "C" sections.

For the preparation of the illustrations in this volume I am most grateful to Betsy Blackwell Williams who devoted much talent and time to photographing the books and consulting with the technicians about the prints.

The assistance I received from Charles Beard and Gerald Becham at the Ina Dillard Russell Library, Georgia College, was generously given, making my research in Milledgeville a most pleasant experience. While in Georgia, I also contacted Leo Zuber, who once edited *The Bulletin*. His was the only complete source of information on Flannery O'Connor's book reviews, and Mr. Zuber was indeed generous in sharing with me all he knew. Also, I am grateful for encouragement in this project from Mrs. Edward F. O'Connor, Robert Giroux, Professor Robert Fitzgerald, and Elizabeth McKee.

Finally, were it not for the wise counsel and guidance of Harry Ransom, Warren Roberts, and William B. Todd and kind personal encouragement from my wife and family, I would not have been able to undertake or complete this task. Any errors which may exist in the bibliography are entirely my own, and in no way do they reflect on the generous assistance given by so many kind people.

INTRODUCTION

It is often difficult to observe trends in an author's publishing career until a descriptive bibliography has been completed, for only then are certain patterns organized and perceptible, and only then is a complete overview of a career possible. Flannery O'Connor's work as a writer is no exception, and this bibliography is offered as such an overview at a time when her reputation as a major force in contemporary Southern literature is stronger than ever before.

Recent events suggest a renewed perception of an already notable career. For instance, in 1977 the Public Broadcasting System first aired an excellent version of "The Displaced Person" as one of nine filmed short stories that comprised the first season of the American Short Story series. Other American writers selected for the series included Sherwood Anderson, Willa Cather, Stephen Crane, William Faulkner, Ernest Hemingway, and Mark Twain. Then, in 1979, a selection of Flannery O'Connor's letters was published as *The Habit of Being*, receiving wide critical acclaim. Fifteen years after her death, the issuing of her letters essentially marked the close of her publishing career, for there is no longer a substantial body of finished writing by O'Connor that remains unpublished. Furthermore, 1980 marked the commercial release of a major motion picture based on the novel *Wise Blood*; produced by Michael and Kathy Fitzgerald and directed by John Huston, "Wise Blood" received highly favorable national notice. Meanwhile, yet another distinction was bestowed on O'Connor—she was the first writer to be named for a special award from the National Book Award Committee. In the past the National Book Awards had gone to single literary works, but in 1980 the Committee took special notice of Flannery O'Connor herself, as an author who in a short career produced a significant body of writing.

Clearly interested in writing at an early age, O'Connor began contributing to the creative writing journal, *The Corinthian*, at Georgia State College for Women as soon as she began her freshman year in 1942. By her senior year she had become its editor. Meanwhile, during the three years in which she completed her degree she contributed linoleum block cartoons to *The Colonnade* (the campus newspaper), *The Alumnae Journal*, *The Corinthian*, and *The Spectrum* (the college yearbook). Her cartoons depict angular figures, at times somewhat grotesque but always wryly humorous. The subject matter of this early published art work naturally centered on college life, and her light-hearted humor also focused on the presence of WAVEs training on campus during the war. In addition, as feature editor for the yearbook during her senior year, O'Connor provided cartoon headpieces which divided the annual into parts and set the overall mood.

Within a year after graduation from GSCW, O'Connor moved to Iowa City to study with Paul Engle at the University of Iowa. Then, in the summer of 1946 she made her first appearance in print in a professional literary forum by publishing "The Geranium" in *Accent*. Stories followed in *The Sewanee Review* and *Mademoiselle* in 1948, *Partisan Review* and *Tomorrow* in 1949, *New World Writing* in 1952, *The Kenyon Review*, *Harper's Bazaar*, and again *The Sewanee Review* in 1953, and, until several years after her death, in these and other journals.

Particularly favored by Catholic colleges and universities, Flannery O'Connor was at times interviewed while on the lecture circuit. Resulting transcripts were published in college literary journals, as in the Spring 1958 *Motley* issued at Spring Hill College, Mobile, Alabama, and the February 1960 issue of *Vagabond* published at Vanderbilt University. Also, for some college journals she would respond to written questions, especially on the art of the short story. Such a reply is found in the Winter 1959 issue of *Esprit*.

Early in 1956 she began reviewing books for *The Bulletin*, a newspaper published by the Catholic Layman's Association of Georgia. In January 1963, when *The Bulletin* split into *The Georgia Bulletin* and *The Southern Cross*, O'Connor continued her reviews in the latter publication, which served the Diocese of Savannah.

Meanwhile, she continued writing short stories and novels. Prior to the completion of both her novels, *Wise Blood* and *The Violent Bear It Away*, parts of them appeared as short stories in *The Partisan Review* and *New World Writing*. Such occurrences are noted in the bibliography.

As a descriptive bibliography of Flannery O'Connor, this work attempts to set forth and describe all her published writings. It includes work published both in her lifetime and posthumously—from the early contributions to journals at Georgia State College for Women, through the stories and books that formed the bulk of the canon, to *The Habit of Being* of 1979. While reprints of O'Connor stories in college texts and anthologies are numerous, they do not fall within the scope of this bibliography since they represent only subsequent printings of her work—printings which were made in most cases with proper permission from the author but without authorial supervision on textual matters. All first appearances of her work, however, are recorded here, whether they came in periodicals, short story anthologies, or her own books. Furthermore, later inclusions of stories by O'Connor in her own books are treated herein.

This bibliography is divided into seven sections, lettered "A" through "G." Section A treats O'Connor's own books and is arranged in chronological order of first appearance. Later editions or impressions of a work appear in chronological "edition families" following the "parent edition." Thus the first edition, first American impression of *Wise Blood* in 1952 is followed by its first English impression (1955), its second American impression (1962), and its second English impression (1968). Next comes the second edition, first American impression.

The system of enumeration employed for books in Section A provides several kinds of information at a glance. For instance, A1.II.a.1 signifies the first title in the section (A1), the second edition (II), the first plating of that edition (a), and the first impression from the plating.[1]

---

[1]Since all of O'Connor's books have been produced in a time when printing by offset lithography is preferred over letterpress, the term "plating" indicates the offset plate prepared for each printing job rather than a stereotype or electrotype plate used in late nineteenth- and early twentieth-century book production.

Each entry in Section A begins with a heading line employing the enumeration system described above; then follow sections on the title, copyright notice, collation, contents, typography and paper, binding, dust jacket, copies examined, and notes. Whenever a page number is followed by a colon in analytical sections of a description, the text directly thereafter is a transcription. Thus, quotation marks are employed in the transcription only when they appear in print in the passage being described.

To measure the terms of an author's popularity with the reading public, it is necessary to know the number of impressions and copies produced for each title. However, descriptive bibliographies have tended to show press run figures only for the first impression of the editions included in the full bibliographical account; therefore, they have not met the needs of scholars requiring more data. This bibliography marks a departure, then, in supplying as much information on later impressions as possible. Unfortunately, dates of publication and figures on all press runs for O'Connor's books are not complete, for in some cases publishers were unwilling to disclose data. Furthermore, in paperback publishing, exact dates of issue are often unknown. Several houses report that they make no attempt to record a day of publication for their paperbacks—to record the month is sufficient for their purposes.

Section B describes the O'Connor contributions to books and pamphlets which are first separate publications of these works. This section is arranged chronologically. Although quasi-facsimile title-page transcriptions are employed in Section B, as in Section A, other aspects of description in Section B have been reduced. For instance, there are no full collations in Section B, and the only contents listed are O'Connor's work in the books.

Section C contains all of Flannery O'Connor's contributions to periodicals (with the exception of brief quotations that sometimes appeared in editors' columns). This section does take into account any complete letters published prior to *The Habit of Being* since these appeared mainly in periodicals (and have been gathered into books as in the case of Stern's *The Books in Fred Hampton's Apartment*). Two unusual aspects of the O'Connor canon recorded in Section C are found in the hitherto-unknown college writings and the little-known but extensive book reviews published in *The Bulletin* and *The Southern Cross*. Unfortunately, I am not able to provide page numbers for references to the reviews since my only source of information has been clippings from the two newspapers in question (clippings that were identified only by date). I have seen a reference to an O'Connor contribution to the *Peabody Palladium*, her high school newspaper; however, no copies are preserved at Georgia College save the two described in Section E.I. Flannery O'Connor's college writings appeared in *The Corinthian*, the creative writing journal at GSCW. Her contributions included essays, book reviews, notes, poems, and stories, some of which display either an eye for incongruity and humor in college life or a definite early ability to deal with the cruel ironies that would form the basis for much of her mature work.

A brief account of miscellaneous appearances in print, Section D, includes a broadside as well as dust-jacket blurbs O'Connor wrote occasionally for books by friends such as J.F. Powers or Richard Stern, while Section E is devoted to the linoleum block cuts O'Connor made for several publications at GSCW during her college years. Most of these lino-cuts, in the form of cartoons with captions appearing in *The Colonnade*, demonstrate a certain wryness or grotesqueness that the author would so accurately display in her writing.

In Section F, I have attempted to account for translations of Flannery O'Connor's works into foreign languages. At times, single stories in translation form only a part of a journal or anthology; on other occasions the entire contents of an O'Connor book comprise a volume in another language. This section may not be complete since there is as yet no definite means of bibliographical control on translations. The *Index Translationum* published by UNESCO provides substantial but incomplete data on translations, and even though I was granted permission to examine contracts relating to foreign editions, it is difficult to tell if an agreement for translation rights indeed resulted in a book.

Section G, the final part of the bibliography, is devoted to adaptations, films, and parodies of O'Connor's works. Although relatively short, this section provides evidence of O'Connor's influence on people working in related creative fields, evidence, for instance, that her stories have an impact and visual imagery that make them appealing to filmmakers. Most notable in this section is the PBS production of "The Displaced Person" starring Irene Worth and John Houseman. Also noteworthy is the film of *Wise Blood* directed by John Huston.

In terms of techniques for descriptive bibliography, some mention should be made of two particular practices within this work. For entries in the A and B sections, reference numbers are employed for colors of ink or binding cloth. ISCC-NBS (Inter Society Color Council, National Bureau of Standards), Centroid Color Charts[2] were used to verify each color, and a number unique to each of 267 named colors is employed in the bibliography. Following each color name (*e.g.,* red-orange), is a number in parentheses (*e.g.,* 34) that refers to a specific color in the ISCC-NBS charts. When the color being identified does not correspond closely with an ISCC color chip, two numbers are used in the parentheses (*e.g.,* 37–34), indicating that the color falls between two ISCC colors and is closest to the number given first.

Another matter concerns the presentation of wording as it appears on bindings and dust jackets. Just as in the sections presenting the quasi-facsimile transcriptions of title pages and copyright notices, the wording on bindings and dust jackets is presented without quotation marks. The colon is employed to signal the beginning of a transcription of actual wording (often accompanied by descriptive elements set off in the traditional manner through italics within square brackets). The close of the transcription of wording is marked with a full stop or a semi-colon. Such punctuation marks following a wording transcription in the sections on bindings and dust jackets should not be considered part of the transcription of actual wording found on the cover of a particular book. There are no instances in the bibliography where the above practices will cause confusion.

For books in the A section, a location symbol is provided for the copies examined. The symbols and their equivalents are as follows:

---

[2]Standard Sample No. 2106 purchased from the National Bureau of Standards. It contains the colorfast chips with identifying numbers used for this bibliography.

GB   George Bixby (personal collection)
EE   Edwin Erbe (personal collection)
DF   David Farmer (personal collection)
GM   Georgia College, Milledgeville (Ina Dillard Russell Library)
TxU   The University of Texas at Austin (Humanities Research Center)

Since this bibliography is concerned with published works only, it does not include a detailed section on manuscripts, which quite clearly represent the pre-publication state of Flannery O'Connor's writings. Most of the manuscript materials have been preserved and are now housed in the Flannery O'Connor Collection at the Ina Dillard Russell Library, Georgia College, Milledgeville.[3]

David Farmer
Tulsa, Oklahoma

---

[3]See Robert J. Dunn, "The Manuscripts of Flannery O'Connor at Georgia College." *The Flannery O'Connor Bulletin,* V (Autumn 1976), 61–69.

Section A
Books

Al. WISE BLOOD

I. FIRST EDITION

a. First Plating (American)

Al.I.a.l

First impression--New York: Harcourt, Brace & Company, 1952

Title: [*on a double spread; pattern of dots*] WISE | NEW
  YORK | | BLOOD | [*pattern of dots*] FLANNERY O'CONNOR |
  HARCOURT, BRACE AND COMPANY | [*pattern of dots*]

Copyright notice: COPYRIGHT, 1949, 1952, BY FLANNERY O'CONNOR |
  ALL RIGHTS RESERVED, INCLUDING THE RIGHT TO REPRODUCE |
  THIS BOOK OR PORTIONS THEREOF IN ANY FORM. | FIRST
  EDITION | LIBRARY OF CONGRESS CATALOG CARD NUMBER 52-6453 |
  PRINTED IN THE UNITED STATES OF AMERICA

Collation: 203 x 133 mm.; [1-6]^{16} [7]^{8} [8]^{16}, 120 leaves;
  pp. [i-ii] [1-8] 9-27 [28] 29-34 [35-36] 37-64 [65-66]
  67-76 [77-78] 79-100 [101-102] 103-115 [116] 117-127
  [128] 129-142 [143-144] 145-162 [163-164] 165-170 [171-
  172] 173-189 [190] 191-198 [199-200] 201-211 [212] 213-
  232 [233-238].

Contents: [i-ii], blank; [1], half-title: WISE BLOOD; [2-3],
  title page; [4], copyright notice; [5]: FOR REGINA; [6],
  blank; [7], fly-title; [8]: CHAPTER 1; 9-27, text; [28]:
  CHAPTER 2; 29-34, text; [35], blank; [36]: CHAPTER 3;
  37-64, text; [65], blank; [66]: CHAPTER 4; 67-76, text;
  [77], blank; [78]: CHAPTER 5; 79-100, text; [101], blank;
  [102]: CHAPTER 6; 103-115, text; [116]: CHAPTER 7; 117-
  127, text; [128]: CHAPTER 8; 129-142, text; [143], blank;
  [144]: CHAPTER 9; 145-162, text; [163], blank; [164]:
  CHAPTER 10; 165-170, text; [171], blank; [172]: CHAPTER
  11; 173-189, text; [190]: CHAPTER 12; 191-198, text;
  [199], blank; [200]: CHAPTER 13; 201-211, text; [212]:
  CHAPTER 14; 213-232, text; [233-238], blank.

Typography and paper: Pagination 4 mm. below text flush right
   (p. 149).   Text--26 lines 151.5 x 93 mm. (p. 57) and 27
   lines 151 x 93 mm. (p. 108).   Paper--white wove; bulk
   18 mm.

Binding: Yellow (83) paper boards with simulated cloth grain.
   Spine printed in brown (81): [*vertical*] WISE [*horizontal*]
   FLANNERY | O'CONNOR [*vertical*] BLOOD [*horizontal*]
   HARCOURT, | BRACE | & COMPANY.   All edges trimmed.   End-
   papers white.

Dust jacket: White printed in red (12) and olive (111) on
   front: [*in olive*] a novel by Flannery O'Connor | [*in white
   centered in pool of red with concentric waves*] WISE |
   [*in pool of olive with concentric waves*] BLOOD; on spine:
   [*olive*] Flannery O'Connor [*red*] WISE BLOOD | [*olive*]
   Harcourt, Brace and Company; on back is a photograph of the
   author; blurbs on flaps, including one by Caroline Gordon.

Copies examined: GB; DF; GM; TxU

Note: Published 15 May 1952 at $3.00.   3000 copies printed.
   Sections of *Wise Blood* were published previously in early
   forms as follows:

   Chapter 1 (pp. 9-27) as "The Train," *The Sewanee Review*
      [C.1948.1]
   Chapter 3 (pp. 37-64) as "The Peeler," *Partisan Review*
      [C.1949.3]
   Chapter 5 (pp. 79-100) as "The Heart of the Park,"
      Partisan Review [C.1949.1]
   Chapter 11 (pp. 173-189) as "Enoch and the Gorilla," *New
      World Writing, First Mentor Selection* [C.1952.1]

Al.I.a.2

Second impression--New York: Farrar, Straus and Cudahy, 1962

Title: [*on a double spread; pattern of dots*] WISE | NEW
   YORK || BLOOD | [*pattern of dots*] FLANNERY O'CONNOR |
   FARRAR, STRAUS AND CUDAHY | [*pattern of dots*]

Copyright notice: COPYRIGHT © 1949, 1952, 1962 BY FLANNERY
   O'CONNOR | LIBRARY OF CONGRESS CATALOG CARD NUMBER
   52-6453 | MANUFACTURED IN THE UNITED STATES OF AMERICA

Collation: 202 x 134 mm.; [1-6]^{16} [7]^{8} [8]^{16}, 120 leaves.

[8]$_{16}$ is blank and pasted down as an endpaper in some
copies. Paging same as in Al.I.a.l except for two fewer
blank pages at end of this impression.

Contents: [i]: BOOKS BY FLANNERY O'CONNOR | *The Violent Bear
It Away* | *A Good Man is Hard to Find* | *Wise Blood*; [ii-l],
title page; [2], copyright notice, [3]: FOR REGINA;
[4], blank; [5]: AUTHOR'S NOTE | TO THE SECOND EDITION |
[*twenty lines of text*]; [6], blank; [7], fly-title; [8]:
CHAPTER 1; 9, text, continuing as in first impression to
232; [233-236], blank.

Typography and paper: Pagination and text same as in first
impression. Paper--white wove; bulk 17 mm.

Binding: Black cloth boards. Spine stamped in gold: FLANNERY |
O'CONNOR WISE BLOOD Farrar, Straus & Cudahy. All edges
trimmed, top edge stained red (27). Endpapers white.

Dust jacket: Designed by Milton Glaser; white printed in black,
red (34), and orange brown (53) on front: [*face with dark
glasses in black on red background*] Flannery O'Connor |
[*in orange brown*] WISE BLOOD; on spine: [*in orange brown*]
Flannery O'Connor | WISE BLOOD [*in black*] Farrar, Straus
& Cudahy; on back are statements by Granville Hicks,
Donald Davidson, and Paul Levine. Blurb on flaps includes
quotations from William Goyen, Caroline Gordon, and Evelyn
Waugh.

Copies examined: GB; DF; GM; TxU

Note: Published 16 August 1962 at $4.50. Another impression
was published in July 1969. This book was produced from
the same setting as the first American and English impressions but contains new material in the form of the
"Author's Note to the Second Edition." *Wise Blood* was
also published as paperback N318 by Noonday Press (a
division of Farrar, Straus & Giroux) in March 1967, with
further impressions in July 1972 and June 1973. The
price of the paperback was $1.95, and it was produced from
the same setting as the Harcourt, the Spearman, and the
other Farrar, Straus & Giroux printings.

I. FIRST EDITION

b. Second plating (English)

Al.I.b.l

First impression--London: Neville Spearman, 1955

Title: [on a double spread; pattern of dots] WISE | LONDON ||
    BLOOD | *[pattern of dots]* FLANNERY O'CONNOR | NEVILLE
    SPEARMAN | *[pattern of dots]*

*Copyright notice: 'Wise Blood' | was first published in 1955
    by | Neville Spearman Limited | 10 Fitzroy Street |
    London W.1 | It was copyright in 1955 by | Flannery
    O'Connor | and was printed in Great Britain by | The
    Hollen Street Press Ltd. | London W.1*

Collation: 196 x 129 mm.; [1-7]^{16} [8]^{4}, 116 leaves. Paging
    same as in Al.I.a.l except there are no blank pages at
    beginning and end.

Contents: [1], half-title: WISE BLOOD; [2-3], title page;
    [4], copyright notice; [5]: FOR REGINA; [6], blank; [7],
    fly-title; [8]: CHAPTER 1; 9, text, continuing as in first
    American impression to 232, but without blank pages at
    end.

Typography and paper: Pagination and text same as in first
    American impression. Paper--white wove; bulk 17 mm.

Binding: Orange (35) paper boards with simulated cloth grain.
    Spine printed in black: *[horizontal]* Wise | Blood |
    [vertical] FLANNERY O'CONNOR | *[horizontal publisher's
    device]* | NEVILLE SPEARMAN. All edges trimmed. Endpapers
    off-white.

Dust jacket: Designed by Guy Nicholls; white printed in black,
    pink (5), and blue (181) on front: *[black and white head
    and hands of praying figure in black hat and blue coat,
    old-fashioned car on pink background]* GUY NICHOLLS | .IT
    IS A REMARKABLE PRODUCT" | *--Evelyn Waugh.* | *[in white]*
    Wise | Blood | *[in black]* FLANNERY | O'CONNOR; on pink
    spine: *[horizontal]* Wise | Blood | *[vertical]* FLANNERY
    O'CONNOR | *[horizontal]* NEVILLE | SPEARMAN; on back is
    photograph and biographical sketch of the author. Blurb
    on front flap includes quotation from Evelyn Waugh;
    advertisements on back flap.

Wise Blood (London: Neville Spearman, 1955): dust jacket (A1.I.b.1)

Copies examined: GB; DF; GM; TxU

Note: Published on 26 June 1955 at 11/6d. 3000 copies were
   printed by the Hollen Street Press, Ltd. This book was
   produced from the same setting as the American impression
   of 1952.

A1.I.b.2

Second impression--London: Faber and Faber, 1968

Title: WISE | BLOOD | FLANNERY O'CONNOR | FABER AND FABER |
   24 Russell Square | London

*Copyright notice: First published in Great Britain in
   mcmlxviii | by Faber and Faber Limited | 24 Russell Square
   London WC1 | Printed in Great Britain by | Latimer Trend &
   Co Ltd Whitstable | All rights reserved | Copyright © 1949,
   1952, 1962 by Flannery O'Connor*

Collation: 196 x 131 mm.; [1-15]^8, 120 leaves. [15]$_8$ is blank
   and pasted down as an endpaper. Paging same as in A1.I.a.2.

Contents: [i], half-title: WISE BLOOD; [ii]: by the same
   author | [*star*] | EVERYTHING THAT RISES MUST CONVERGE;
   [1], title page; [2], copyright notice; [3]: FOR REGINA;
   [4], blank; [5]: AUTHOR'S NOTE | TO THE SECOND EDITION
   (1962); [6], blank; [7], fly-title; [8]: CHAPTER 1; 9,
   text, continuing as in first American impression to 232;
   [233-236], blank.

Typography and paper: Pagination and text same as first
   American impression. Paper--white wove; bulk 15 mm.

Binding: Red (12) cloth boards. Spine stamped in gold:
   WISE | BLOOD | [*bullet*] | Flannery | O'Connor | Faber.
   All edges trimmed. Endpapers white.

Dust jacket: White printed in black, orange (35), and red (13);
   on front: [*on orange background in white*] Wise |
   [*red*] Wise | [*white*] Blood | [*red*] Blood [*in black,
   vertically near outer edge*] Flannery O'Connor; on spine
   of orange background: [*white*] Wise | Blood | [*vertically,
   red*] Flannery O'Connor | [*horizontally, black*] FABER;
   advertisements on back; blurb on front flap for *Wise
   Blood*, on back flap for *Everything That Rises Must Converge* containing quotation from V.S. Pritchett.

Copies examined: GB; DF; GM; TxU

Note: Published by Faber and Faber on 29 January 1968 at 25s.
3000 copies were printed by Latimer Trend & Co. This is
the same setting used in the Farrar, Straus and Cudahy
and the Neville Spearman printings. Similar use of the
last leaf in the final gathering as a paste-down endpaper
occurs here as in the second American impression. Faber
and Faber reissued *Wise Blood* in 1980 with a new introduction by V.S. Pritchett, too late for inclusion in the
bibliography.

II. SECOND EDITION

a. First Plating (American)

A1.II.a.1

First impression--New York: The New American Library, 1953

Title: WISE BLOOD | by | Flannery O'Connor | [*publisher's
device*] | A SIGNET BOOK | Published by THE NEW AMERICAN
LIBRARY

Copyright notice: COPYRIGHT, 1949, 1952, BY FLANNERY
O'CONNOR | All rights reserved, including the right to
repro- | duce this book or portions thereof in any form. |
Published as a SIGNET BOOK | *By Arrangement with Harcourt,
Brace and Company* | FIRST PRINTING, JUNE, 1953 | [*next 3
lines within ruled box*] SIGNET BOOKS are published by |
The New American Library of World Literature, Inc. | 501
Madison Avenue, New York 22, New York | PRINTED IN THE
UNITED STATES OF AMERICA

Collation: 182 x 110 mm.; perfect binding, 72 leaves; pp. [1-
6] 7-143 [144].

Contents: [1], blurbs; [2], advertisements; [3], title page;
[4], copyright notice; [5]: FOR REGINA; [6], blank;
7-[144], text; [144], advertisements below text. Chapter
heads and text begin on 7, 20, 24, 43, 50, 65, 73, 81,
90, 102, 106, 118, 123, and 131.

Typography and paper: Pagination centered 14 mm. above base
of page (p. 25). Text--39 lines 151 x 90 mm. (p. 47).
Paper--white wove; bulk 8 mm.

Binding: Stiff white paper wrappers. On front is band in
    orange (68) in which is printed in black: 1029 | A
    Searching Novel of Sin and Redemption | [*publisher's
    device with price of 25 cents*] | [*picture in shades of
    green, grey, brown, and red of woman lifting hat from face
    of man lying in grass, tree with jay at top, mountain,
    shack, and car in background; at top of picture in red
    (17)*] Wise Blood | [*in black*] FLANNERY O'CONNOR | [*band
    of black at base printed in white*] A SIGNET BOOK | Complete
    and Unabridged; on spine: [*in black on orange*] 1029 |
    [*vertical*] WISE BLOOD FLANNERY O'CONNOR; back cover with
    orange and white section printed in black and red (11),
    also picture of author and brief biographical sketch.
    All edges trimmed and stained red (11).

Copies examined: GB; DF

Note: Published in May 1953 at 25¢. 234,090 copies were
    printed.

III. THIRD EDITION

a. First Plating (English)

A1.III.a.1

First impression--London: Harborough Publishing Company, 1960

Title: WISE BLOOD | FLANNERY O'CONNOR | THE HARBOROUGH
    PUBLISHING CO. LTD., | 44 BEDFORD ROW, LONDON W.C.1

Copyright notice: Bound edition first published in England
    in 1955 by | Neville Spearman Limited, London, W.1 |
    © 1955 by Flannery O'Connor | All rights reserved | First
    Ace Books edition 1960 | FOR REGINA | Printed in Great
    Britain by | Cox & Wyman Ltd., London, Reading and
    Fakenham

Collation: 177 x 113 mm.; perfect binding, 80 leaves;
    pp. [1-4] 5-154 [155-160].

Contents: [1], half-title: WISE BLOOD; [2], advertisements
    for other Ace books by Arthur Miller, Truman Capote, and
    J.D. Salinger; [3], title page; [4], copyright notice;
    5-154, text, with chapter heads and text beginning on 5,

19, 24, 44, 52, 68, 78, 86, 96, 109, 113, 126, 132, and
141; [155-160], advertisements.

Typography and paper: Pagination centered 13 mm. above base
    of page (p. 25).   Text--36 lines 151 x 89 mm.   Paper--
    white wove; bulk 11 mm.

Binding: Stiff white paper wrappers. On front: [*printed in
    white in a black ace of spades*] ACE | BOOKS | [*in black*]
    H348 [*price 2/6 in circle*] | [*in red (11)*)] WISE | BLOOD
    A BRUTAL, PASSIONATE NOVEL OF SIN AND | REDEMPTION IN A
    SOUTHERN TOWN | [*in black*] FLANNERY O'CONNOR; on lower
    half of upper wrapper is an illustration in shades of
    pink, orange, blue, and brown of a blonde woman in black
    slip seated on a brass bed, a man clothed in denim shirt
    and trousers stands in partly open door, room furnished
    with a pot-belly stove, kerosene lamp on cloth-covered
    table; on black spine: [*white ace of spades with black
    lettering*] ACE | BOOKS | [*vertical in white*] WISE BLOOD
    FLANNERY O'CONNOR | [*horizontal*] H348; on back: [*in red
    (13)*)] WISE BLOOD | [*in black*] Flannery O'Connor | [*4
    testimonials in black, headlined in red*] | [*photograph
    of author in black; in blue (178-182) on either side*]
    ACE | BOOKS. All edges trimmed.

Copies examined: EE; GM

Note: Published in 1960 at 2/6d from a new setting of type.

                    FOURTH EDITION

                    (*see* A4.I.a.1)

A2. A GOOD MAN IS HARD TO FIND

I. FIRST EDITION

a. First Plating (American)

A2.I.a.1

First impression--New York: Harcourt, Brace and Company, 1955

Title: [*on a double spread*] A GOOD MAN IS | *Also by Flannery*
   O'Connor: WISE BLOOD || *Flannery O'Connor* | HARD TO FIND |
   AND OTHER STORIES | *Harcourt, Brace and Company* | *New York*

Copyright notice: © COPYRIGHT, 1953, 1954, 1955 BY FLANNERY
   O'CONNOR | *All rights reserved, including* | *the right to*
   reproduce this book | *or portions thereof in any form.* |
   first edition | LIBRARY OF CONGRESS CATALOG CARD NUMBER:
   55-7423 | PRINTED IN THE UNITED STATES OF AMERICA

Collation: 202.5 x 134.5 mm.; [1-8]^{16}, 128 leaves; pp. [1-9]
   10-29 [30] 31-52 [53] 54-68 [69] 70-84 [85] 86-101 [102]
   103-129 [130] 131-154 [155] 156-168 [169] 170-196 [197]
   198-251 [252-256].

Contents: [1], half-title: A GOOD MAN IS HARD TO FIND; [2-3],
   title page; [4], copyright notice; [5]: FOR SALLY AND
   ROBERT FITZGERALD; [6], blank; [7], table of contents;
   [8], blank; [9]-251, text, each story with head-title
   beginning on unnumbered page as below; pp. [252-256],
   blank.

   [9]-29 "A Good Man Is Hard to Find" first appeared in
   The Avon Book of Modern Writing, William Phillips and
   Philip Rahv, eds. New York: Avon Publications, Inc.,
   1953. Pp. 186-199. [B2]
   [30]-52 "The River" first appeared in *The Sewanee Re-*
   view, 61, No. 3 (Summer 1953), 455-475. [C.1953.2]
   [53]-68 "The Life You Save May Be Your Own" first
   appeared in *The Kenyon Review*, 15, No. 2 (Spring 1953),
   195-207. [C.1953.1]
   [69]-84 "A Stroke of Good Fortune" first appeared in an
   earlier version as "The Woman on the Stairs" in *Tomor-*
   row, 8, No. 12 (August 1949), 40-44; under the present
   title it first appeared in *Shenandoah*, 4, No. 1 (Spring
   1953), 7-18. [C.1949.2]

[85]-101 "A Temple of the Holy Ghost" first appeared in
Harper's Bazaar, 88, No. 2910 (May 1954), 108-109, 162-
164, 169. [C.1954.2]

[102]-129 "The Artificial Nigger" first appeared in *The
Kenyon Review*, 17, No. 2 (Spring 1955), 169-192.
[C.1955.1]

[130]-154 "A Circle in the Fire" first appeared in *The
Kenyon Review*, 16, No. 2 (Spring 1954), 169-190.
[C.1954.1]

[155]-168 "A Late Encounter with the Enemy" first appeared in *Harper's Bazaar*, 87 (September 1953), 234,
247, 249, 252. [C.1953.3]

[169]-196 "Good Country People" also appeared in *Harper's
Bazaar*, 89, No. 2923 (June 1955), 64-65, 116-117, 121-
122, 124, 130. [C.1955.2]

[197]-251 "The Displaced Person" first appeared in *The
Sewanee Review*, 62, No. 4 (Autumn 1954), 634-654.
[C.1954.3]

Typography and paper: Pagination 2.5 mm. above text flush with
outer margins (p. 107). Running head: FLANNERY O'CONNOR,
in all caps Roman on all text versos except when they
contain beginning of a new story. New chapter titles in
all caps Roman. Running heads (title of story) in cap
and lower case italic on all text rectos except when they
contain beginning of a new story. Text--32 lines 151 x
97 mm. (p. 66). Paper--white wove; bulk 19 mm.

Binding: Black paper boards with simulated cloth grain. Spine
printed in orange-yellow (67) and pink (248): [*vertical
in orange-yellow*] *Flannery O'Connor* | [*horizontal in pink*]
A | GOOD | MAN | IS | HARD | TO | FIND | [*vertical in
orange-yellow*] *Harcourt, Brace and Company.* All edges
trimmed. Endpapers white.

Dust jacket: Designed by Halmerson; white printed in red (12)
and orange-yellow (72), front and spine of orange-yellow
background; on front: [*in red*] FLANNERY O'CONNOR | [*in
white*] author of WISE BLOOD | [*in areas of red for each
word with white solid lines and red dotted lines echoing
shape of each area*] A Good Man | Is Hard to Find; on spine
in white: [*vertical*] FLANNERY | O'CONNOR | [*horizontal on
red background*] *Harcourt,* | *Brace and* | *Company* | [*vertical
on gold background*] A Good Man | Is Hard to Find; on back
in red are statements by Caroline Gordon, William Goyen,
Sylvia Stallings, Evelyn Waugh, and others; blurb for *A
Good Man Is Hard to Find* on both flaps, biographical
sketch of author on back flap.

Copies examined: GB; DF; GM; TxU

Note: Published 12 May 1955 at $3.50. 2500 copies were
   printed. Subsequent reprints include the second printing
   of 1500 copies on 28 June 1955, the third printing of 1500
   copies on 14 September 1955, the fourth printing of 1000
   copies on 18 June 1956, the fifth printing of 1000 copies
   on 6 October 1961 (with a price change to $3.75), the
   sixth printing of 2000 copies on 22 December 1964 (with
   a price change to $3.95), the seventh printing of 1500
   copies on 11 March 1966, the eighth printing of 1000
   copies on 28 May 1968 (with a price change to $4.50),
   and the ninth printing of 1000 copies on 26 June 1972
   (with a price change to $5.95). In all, Harcourt, Brace
   produced 13,000 copies of the book between 1955 and 1972.
   In autumn 1977 Harcourt Brace Jovanovich issued a Harvest
   paperback at $3.45.

I. FIRST EDITION

b. Second Plating (English)

A2.I.b.1

First impression--London: Neville Spearman, 1957

Title: THE | *Artificial* | *Nigger* | AND OTHER TALES | *by* |
   FLANNERY O'CONNOR | LONDON | *Neville* | *Spearman*

Copyright notice: 'The Artificial Nigger' | *was first*
   published in 1957 *by* | *Neville Spearman Limited* | 112
   Whitfield Street | *London, W.1* | *All rights reserved* |
   It was printed in Great Britain by | *D. R. Hillman &*
   Sons Ltd., Frome

Collation: 194 x 129 mm.; [A]^{16} B-H^{16}, 128 leaves. H$_{16}$ is
   blank and pasted down as an endpaper. Pagination same
   as A2.I.a.1 except for two fewer blank pages at end of
   this impression.

Contents: [1], half-title: THE ARTIFICIAL NIGGER; [2], blank;
   [3], title page; [4], copyright notice; [5], dedication:
   FOR SALLY AND ROBERT FITZGERALD; [6], blank; [7], table
   of contents; [8], blank; [9], text, continuing as in first
   American impression to 251; [252-254], blank.

The Artificial Nigger (London: Neville Spearman, 1957): dust jacket (A2.I.b.1)

Typography and paper: Pagination same as first American im-
    pression. Text--32 lines 150 x 96.5 mm. (p. 66). Paper--
    white wove; bulk 16.5 mm.

Binding: Orange-pink (27) paper boards with simulated cloth
    grain. Spine stamped in gold: THE | ARTIFICIAL | NIGGER |
    [*star*] FLANNERY | O'CONNOR | NEVILLE | SPEARMAN. All
    edges trimmed. Endpapers white.

Dust jacket: White printed in brown (47) and red (34). On
    front, photograph of shoulders and uplifted head of Negro
    man, over which printed in red: *Flannery* | *O'Connor* |
    The | *Artificial* | *Nigger* | *and other tales;* on spine in
    white: [*vertical*] *O'Connor   The Artificial Nigger
    Spearman;* on back in brown is photograph of the author
    and advertisement for *Wise Blood;* blurb on front flap
    about *The Artificial Nigger,* on back flap advertisements
    for other Spearman books.

Copies examined: GB; DF; TxU

Note: Published 27 September 1957 at 13/6d. 2000 copies were
    printed by D.R. Hillman & Sons.

I. FIRST EDITION

c. Third Plating (English)

A2.I.c.1

Second impression--London: Faber and Faber, 1968

Title: [*on a double spread*] A GOOD MAN IS || *Flannery*
    O'Connor | HARD TO FIND | AND OTHER STORIES | *Faber and*
    Faber Limited, | *24 Russell Square,* | *London.*

Copyright notice: First published in England in mcmlxviii |
    by Faber and Faber Limited | *24 Russell Square London*
    WC1 | *Printed in Great Britain by* | *Latimer Trend & Co*
    Ltd Whitstable | *All rights reserved* | © COPYRIGHT, 1953,
    1954, 1955, 1957 and 1968, | BY FLANNERY O'CONNOR

Collation: 200 x 131 mm.; [1-16]^8, 128 leaves. [16]$_8$ is blank
    and pasted down as an endpaper. Pagination same as
    A2.I.b.1.

Contents: [1], half-title: A GOOD MAN IS HARD TO FIND; [2-3],
title page; [4], copyright notice; [5], dedication: FOR
SALLY AND ROBERT FITZGERALD; [6], blank; [7], table of
contents; [8], blank; [9], text, continuing as in first
American impression to 251; [252-254], blank.

Typography and paper: Pagination and text same as first
American impression. Paper--white wove; bulk 17 mm.

Binding: Red (12) cloth boards. Stamped on spine in gold:
A | GOOD | MAN | IS | HARD | TO | FIND | [*circle*]
Flannery | O'Connor | FABER. All edges trimmed. End-
papers white.

Dust jacket: White printed in blue (177); on front over blue
background: [*in white*] Flannery O'Connor | [*rule*] | [*in
black decorative letters*] A GOOD | MAN | IS HARD | TO
FIND; on blue spine: [*vertical in white*] Flannery O'Connor
[*in black*] A Good Man is Hard to Find [*horizontal*] FABER;
on back, advertisements for one work by Sylvia Plath and
two by Denton Welch. Blurb on front flap concerns *A Good
Man Is Hard to Find*, on back flap blurbs for *Wise Blood*
and *Everything That Rises Must Converge.*

Copies examined: GB; DF; GM; TxU

Note: Published 3 September 1968 at 25s. 2500 copies were
printed by Latimer Trend & Company. Also, from this
setting another English edition was published in 1980 by
the Women's Press with an introduction by Lisa Alther;
price, £7.50.

II. SECOND EDITION

a. First Plating (American)

A2.II.a.1

First impression--New York: The New American Library, 1956

Title: A GOOD MAN | IS HARD TO FIND | *and other stories* | by
FLANNERY O'CONNOR | [*publisher's device*] | A SIGNET
BOOK | Published by THE NEW AMERICAN LIBRARY

Copyright notice: © COPYRIGHT, 1953, 1954, 1955, BY FLANNERY
O'CONNOR | All rights reserved, including | the right to

reproduce this book │ or portions thereof in any form. │
Published as a SIGNET BOOK │ By Arrangement with Harcourt,
Brace and Company │ <u>FIRST PRINTING</u>, OCTOBER, 1956 │
[*rule*] │ FOR SALLY AND ROBERT FITZGERALD │ [*rule*] │ [*next*
3 lines within ruled box] SIGNET BOOKS are published by │
The New American Library of World Literature, Inc. │ 501
Madison Avenue, New York 22, New York │ <u>PRINTED IN THE</u>
<u>UNITED STATES OF AMERICA</u>

Collation: 178 x 106 mm.; perfect binding, 96 leaves; pp. [1-
7] 8-190 [191-192].

Contents: [1], advertisement for *A Good Man Is Hard to Find*
and note on reprint status; [2], other advertisements;
[3], title page; [4], copyright notice; [5], table of
contents; [6], blank; [7], text, continuing to 190;
stories in same order as first edition begin on [7], 23,
41, 53, 66, 79, 100, 119, 129, and 150; [191-192], advertisements.

Typography and paper: Pagination 3 mm. above type, flush with
outer margins (p. 147); centered 2 mm. below bottom line
on opening page of each story (p. 79). Running head:
FLANNERY O'CONNOR, in all caps Roman on all text versos
except at beginning of each new story. New chapter titles
in all caps Roman. Running head (title of story) in cap
and lower case italics on all rectos except when they
contain beginning of a new story. Text--44 lines 153 x
87 mm. (p. 115). Paper--white wove; bulk 13.7 mm.

Binding: Stiff white paper wrappers. Printed on front: [*to*
left in black] S1345 │ [*Signet device with price of 35¢*
reversed in background color; to right] "Highly
unladylike ... a brutal irony, │ a slam-bang humor and a
style of writing │ as balefully direct as a death
sentence." │ --*Time* Magazine │ [*drawing in tones of brown,*
grey, red, and white of man and woman struggling beside
open briefcase with bottle in it, a pitchfork behind
them] │ [*in red (11)*] A Good Man │ Is Hard to Find │ [*in*
lower right corner, drawing in tones of grey, brown, and
black of a river baptism with mother, child, and preacher;
to left in black] FLANNERY O'CONNOR │ One of the Freshest
and │ Most Highly Acclaimed │ New Talents │ [*in red*] A
SIGNET BOOK │ Complete and Unabridged; printed on spine
in black on brownish pink (near 33) background: [*horizontal*] S │ 1345 │ [*vertical*] A GOOD MAN IS HARD TO FIND
Flannery O'Connor; back cover printed in red and black on
brownish pink and yellow (near 84) background with adver-

A Good Man Is Hard to Find (New York: The New American Library, 1956): front and back covers (A2.II.a.1)

tisement for *A Good Man Is Hard to Find* as well as biographical note and half-tone photograph of the author.
All edges trimmed and stained red (11).

Copies examined: GB; TxU

Note: Published in October 1956 at 35¢. 173,750 copies were
printed. A second printing of this edition was issued in
April 1961 at 50¢ as Signet #D1965. 41,117 copies of the
second printing were produced, and a new wrapper was
designed with a water-color drawing of three gangsters
on the upper cover, the center figure without a shirt.

II. SECOND EDITION

b. Second Plating (English)

A2.II.b.1

First impression--London: The New English Library, 1962

Title: A GOOD MAN IS | HARD TO FIND | *FLANNERY O'CONNOR* |
[*publisher's device*] | THE NEW ENGLISH LIBRARY LTD.

Copyright notice: First published in England by Neville
Spearman Ltd. in 1957 under the title *The* | *Artificial
Nigger* | © Copyright 1953, 1954, 1955 by Flannery
O'Connor | All rights reserved | [*star*] | FIRST FOUR
SQUARE EDITION 1962 | *For Sally and Robert Fitzgerald* |
Conditions of Sale: This book shall not, without the
written consent of the publishers | first given, be lent,
re-sold, hired out or otherwise disposed of by way of
trade in any | form of binding or cover other than that
in which it is published. | *Four Square Books are
published by The New English Library Limited from
Barnard's Inn,* | *Holborn, London EC1. They are made
and printed in Great Britain by Love and* | *Malcomson Ltd,
Redhill, Surrey*

Collation: 181 x 107 mm.; perfect binding, 96 leaves; pp. [1-
7] 8-190 [191-192].

Contents: [1], half-title: A GOOD MAN IS HARD TO FIND;
[2]: [*star*] | *Also available in the Four Square series:* |
FOR ESMÉ---WITH LOVE AND SQUALOR | J.D. Salinger | The
impulses of childhood and adolescence, | by the author of

A Good Man Is Hard to Find (London: The New English Library, 1962): front and back covers (A2.II.b.1)

The Catcher in the Rye. | 2s. 6d.; [3], title page; [4],
copyright notice; [5], text, continuing to 190 as in
American edition; [191-192], advertisements.

Typography and paper: Pagination and text same as in American
plating. Paper--white wove; bulk 11 mm.

Binding: Stiff white paper wrappers. Printed on front:
[*publisher's device in black and red-orange (near 34)*] |
[*in black*] 2/6 FLANNERY O'CONNOR | [*in red*] One of the
freshest and most | highly acclaimed talents of | our
time | [*in black*] A | GOOD MAN | IS | HARD TO | FIND |
[*on lower half a color drawing of 3 men in front of a
tree, center one with open shirt and carrying rifle, outer
figures hold pistols; man on right in pink (2-5) T-shirt*];
on spine: [*reading across, publisher's device in black
and red-orange on white background; on red-orange ground
reading down in black*] A GOOD MAN IS HARD TO FIND Flannery
O'Connor | [*in black on white ground reading across*] 676;
on back, blurbs, biographical sketch, and publisher's
name and device in black, red-orange, and blue (178-182).
All edges trimmed.

Copy examined: DF

Note: Published in July 1962 at 2/6d. 10,000 copies were
printed by Love and Malcomson.

THIRD EDITION

(*see* A4.I.a.1)

IV. FOURTH EDITION

a. First Plating (American)

A2.IV.a.1

First impression--Garden City: Image Books, 1970

Title: FLANNERY O'CONNOR | A Good Man | Is Hard to Find |
AND OTHER STORIES | [*publisher's device to left of next
three lines*] IMAGE BOOKS | *A Division of Doubleday &
Company, Inc.* | *Garden City, New York*

Copyright notice: Image Books edition 1970 | by special
    arrangement with Harcourt, Brace & World, Inc. | Image
    Books edition published September 1970 | Copyright © 1953,
    1954, 1955 by Flannery O'Connor | All Rights Reserved |
    Printed in the United States of America

Collation: 180 x 106 mm.; perfect binding, 120 leaves; pp. [1-
    11] 12-29 [30-31] 32-51 [52-53] 54-66 [67] 68-81 [82-83]
    84-97 [98-99] 100-123 [124-125] 126-146 [147] 148-158
    [159] 160-183 [184-185] 186-233 [234-240].

Contents: [1], blurbs; [2], blank; [3], title page; [4], copy-
    right notice; [5]: FOR SALLY AND ROBERT FITZGERALD; [6]:
    Other Books by Flannery O'Connor | WISE BLOOD | THE VIOLENT
    BEAR IT AWAY | EVERYTHING THAT RISES MUST CONVERGE | THREE
    (contains: WISE BLOOD, | THE VIOLENT BEAR IT AWAY, and |
    A GOOD MAN IS HARD TO FIND); [7], table of contents; [8],
    blank; [9], fly-title; [10], blank; [11], text, continuing
    to 233 with stories in same order as first edition begin-
    ning on [11], [31], [53], [67], [83], [99], [125], [147],
    [159], and [185]; [30], [52], [82], [98], [124], and [184]
    blank; [234-240], advertisements.

Typography and paper: Pagination 3.7 mm. (p. 169) above type,
    flush with outer margins of type page. Running head:
    FLANNERY O'CONNOR in all caps Roman flush right on all
    text versos except blank pages. New chapter titles flush
    right in all caps Roman. Running head (title of story)
    in cap and lower case italics flush left on all text
    rectos except when they contain beginning of a new story.
    Text--37 lines 141 x 83 mm. (p. 126); occasionally 38 lines
    (p. 197). Paper--white wove; bulk 13 mm.

Binding: Stiff paper wrappers. Printed as background of
    front and spine is photograph of wood lapboard siding
    over which is printed (on upper cover): A DOUBLEDAY IMAGE
    BOOK $1.25 | ORIGINAL EDITION $4.50 | [*in green (131)*]
    Flannery O'Connor | [*in brown (43)*] A Good | Man Is | Hard
    To | Find | [*in black*] TEN MEMORABLE SHORT STORIES |
    COMPLETE AND UNABRIDGED | [*in green*] IMAGE D279 [*publisher's
    device*]; on spine: [*horizontal*] $1.25 | [*vertical, in
    brown*] A Good Man Is Hard To Find [*in green*] Flannery |
    O'Connor | [*horizontal, in black*] IMAGE | D279; on back,
    two statements in black, title of book and publisher
    printed in green. All edges trimmed.

Copies examined: GB; DF; TxU

Note: Published 9 September 1970 at $1.25. 10,000 copies
   were printed. A second impression of 10,000 copies was
   issued on 26 August 1971 at the same price.

A3. THE VIOLENT BEAR IT AWAY

I. FIRST EDITION

a. First Plating (American)

A3.I.a.1

First impression--New York: Farrar, Straus and Cudahy, 1960

Title: [*on a double spread*] "FROM THE DAYS OF JOHN | THE
   KINGDOM OF HEAVEN | AND THE VIOLENT BEAR IT | The violent
   bear | FLANNERY O'CONNOR || THE BAPTIST UNTIL NOW, |
   SUFFERETH VIOLENCE, | AWAY." Matthew 11:12 | it away |
   New York: Farrar, Straus & Cudahy

Copyright notice: Copyright © 1955, 1960 by Flannery O'Connor |
   Library of Congress Catalog Number: 60-6752 | *Manufactured
   in the United States of America* | *by H. Wolff, New York*

Collation: 202 x 133 mm.; [1-8]^{16}, 128 leaves; pp. [i-x] [1-3]
   4-52 [53] 54-84 [85] 86-93 [94-97] 98-118 [119] 120-137
   [138-139] 140-147 [148-149] 150-157 [158-159] 160-177
   [178-179] 180-203 [204-207] 208-218 [219] 220-233 [234-
   235] 236-243 [244-246].

Contents: [i], half-title: THE VIOLENT BEAR IT AWAY; [ii],
   blank; [iii]: *Books by Flannery O'Connor* | WISE BLOOD |
   A GOOD MAN IS HARD TO FIND | THE VIOLENT BEAR IT AWAY;
   [iv-v], title page; [vi], copyright notice; [vii]: For
   Edward Francis O'Connor | 1896-1941; [viii], blank; [ix],
   section contents: ONE : 1 | TWO : 95 | THREE : 205; [x],
   blank; [1], divisional half-title: ONE; [2], blank; [3]-
   52, chapter I; [53]-84, chapter II; [85]-93, chapter III;
   [94], blank; [95], divisional half-title: TWO; [96],
   blank; [97]-118, chapter IV; [119]-137, chapter V; [138],
   blank; [139]-147, chapter VI; [148], blank; [149]-157,
   chapter VII; [158], blank; [159]-177, chapter VIII; [178],
   blank; [179]-203, chapter IX; [204], blank; [205],

divisional half-title: THREE; [206], blank; [207]-218,
chapter X; [219]-233, chapter XI; [234], blank; [235]-
243, chapter XII; [244-246], blank.

Typography and paper: Pagination followed by a colon 6.5 mm.
above text flush left (p. 120). Chapters begin with
Roman chapter number half way down page set flush left,
5.5 mm. above first line of text (p. [159]). Text--29
lines 148.5 x 88.5 mm. (p. 70) and 149 x 89 mm. (p. 113).
Paper--white wove; bulk 20 mm.

Binding: Grey (192) half-cloth with red (12-13) paper boards
with simulated batik wrinkle pattern. Spine printed in
white, grey (264), and medium grey (265): The | violent |
bear it | away | [*in grey*] FLANNERY | O'CONNOR | [*in
medium grey*] FARRAR | STRAUS & | CUDAHY. All edges
trimmed, top edges stained grey (266). Endpapers black.

Dust jacket: Designed by Milton Glaser; white printed in
purple (223), yellow (83), brown (54), and black; on front:
[*in yellow*] FLANNERY O'CONNOR | [*in black*] A novel by the
author of *A Good Man is Hard to Find* | [*in white*] THE
VIOLENT BEAR IT AWAY | [*in black, face of a boy in hat
looking through brown plants, all on a purple background*];
on spine of purple: [*in yellow*] FLANNERY | O'CONNOR |
[*vertical in black*] THE VIOLENT BEAR IT AWAY | [*horizontal*]
FSC; on back, 20-line statement by Caroline Gordon about
the author. Blurbs on flaps include quotations from
Granville Hicks and Orville Prescott as well as biographical
sketch of the author.

Copies examined: GB; DF; TxU

Note: Published 8 February 1960 at $3.75. Printed by H. Wolff.
A second impression of this edition was published by
Farrar, Straus & Giroux in March 1966 and a third in April
1968, both for $4.95. The title page was redesigned for
these impressions to a single page as follows: THE
VIOLENT | BEAR IT AWAY | FLANNERY O'CONNOR | *Farrar,
Straus & Giroux New York* [*device*]. These later printings
are bound in red (near 12) cloth boards printed in black.
The top edges of the second impression are white, but for
the third impression they are stained black. The dust
jackets have the same design as on the first American
impression but with some changes in the blurbs. Noonday
Press, the paperback division of Farrar, Straus & Giroux,
issued the novel (N303) in wrappers in March 1966, April
1968, July 1969, January and August 1970, and September

1972. The first part of *The Violent Bear It Away* was
published previously in the following early form:

Chapter 1 (pp. [3]-52)--"You Can't Be Any Poorer Than
    Dead," *New World Writing*, No. 8 (October 1955), 81-97.
    [C.1955.3]

I. FIRST EDITION

b. Second Plating (English)

A3.I.b.1

First impression--London: Longmans, Green and Company, 1960

Title: [*on a double spread*] 'From the days of John the Baptist
    until now, | The Kingdom of Heaven suffereth violence and
    the | violent bear it away.' Matthew II : 12 | The
    violent bear | FLANNERY O'CONNOR || it away | *Longmans*

Copyright notice: LONGMANS, GREEN AND CO LTD | 6 & 7 CLIFFORD
    STREET, LONDON WI | [*13 lines listing Longmans' foreign
    offices*] | *Copyright © 1955, 1960 by Flannery O'Connor* |
    This edition first published 1960 | Printed in Great
    Britain by | Lowe and Brydone (Printers) Limited, London,
    N.W.10

Collation: 195.5 x 128.5 mm.; [A]^8 B-Q^8, 128 leaves; pagination
    same as in first American impression.

Contents: [i], half-title: THE VIOLENT BEAR IT AWAY; [ii],
    blank; [iii]: *Books by Flannery O'Connor* | WISE BLOOD |
    THE ARTIFICIAL NIGGER; [iv-v], title page; [vi], copyright
    notice; [vii], dedication: For Edward Francis O'Connor |
    1896-1941; [viii], blank; [ix], section contents:
    ONE : 1 | TWO : 95 | THREE : 205; [x], blank; [1], divi-
    sional half-title: ONE; [2], blank; [3], text, continuing
    to 243 as in first American impression; [244-246], blank.

Typography and paper: Pagination and text same as in first
    American impression. Paper--white wove; bulk 17.5 mm.

Binding: Orange (34) paper boards with simulated cloth grain.
    Spine stamped in gold: *The* | *Violent* | *Bear It* | *Away* |
    [*asterisk*] | FLANNERY | O'CONNOR | *Longmans*. All edges
    trimmed. Endpapers white. In addition, a binding variant
    in red paper boards is reported by George Bixby.

Dust jacket: White printed in black, orange (35), violet (211),
   and reddish brown (44); on front, purple barn and wagon,
   figure in black against orange background wearing hat and
   holding double-barrelled shotgun: [*in black*] the | [*in
   white*] Violent | bear | it | away | [*in black*] Flannery
   O'Connor; on spine, boy in purple, orange, and reddish
   brown wearing coveralls: [*in black*] the | Violent | bear |
   it | away | Flannery | O'Connor | LONGMANS; on back,
   advertisement for *The Cactus Grove* by Michel Landa.
   Following blurb is biographical sketch of the author.

Copies examined: GB; DF; GM; TxU

Note: Published 12 September 1960 at 16/-.   3500 copies were
   printed by Lowe and Brydone.

I. FIRST EDITION

c. Third Plating (English)

A3.I.c.1

First impression--London: Faber and Faber, 1969

Title: THE VIOLENT | BEAR IT AWAY | FLANNERY O'CONNOR | FABER
   AND FABER | 24 Russell Square, London

*Copyright notice: First published in England 1960 | by
   Longmans, Green & Co | Reissued 1969 | by Faber and Faber
   Limited | 24 Russell Square London WC1 | Printed in Great
   Britain by | Latimer Trend & Co Ltd Whitstable | All
   rights reserved | SBN 571 08771 X | Copyright © 1955,
   1960 by Flannery O'Connor*

Collation: 200 x 132 mm.; [1]^8 (±1$_3$) [2-16]^8, 128 leaves;
   pagination same as in first American impression.

Contents: [i], half-title: THE VIOLENT BEAR IT AWAY; [ii]:
   Books by Flannery O'Connor | WISE BLOOD | A GOOD MAN IS
   HARD TO FIND | EVERYTHING THAT RISES MUST CONVERGE;
   [iii]: *"FROM THE DAYS OF JOHN THE BAPTIST | UNTIL NOW,
   THE KINGDOM OF HEAVEN | SUFFERETH VIOLENCE, AND THE
   VIOLENT | BEAR IT AWAY."* Matthew 11:12; [iv], blank;
   [v], title page; [vi], copyright notice; [vii]-[246], as
   in first English impression.

Typography and paper: Pagination and text same as in first
    American and English impressions. Paper--white wove;
    bulk 17 mm.

Binding: Red (13) cloth boards. Spine stamped in gold:
    The | Violent | bear it | away | FLANNERY O'CONNOR |
    FABER. All edges trimmed. Endpapers white.

Dust jacket: White printed in black and pink (27); on front,
    on pink background: [*in white*] Flannery O'Connor | [*rule*] |
    [*in black*] The | Violent | Bear | It | Away; on spine of
    pink background: [*vertical in white*] Flannery O'Connor
    [*in black*] The Violent Bear It Away [*horizontal*] FABER;
    on back, advertisements for *A Good Man Is Hard to Find*,
    Everything That Rises Must Converge, and *Wise Blood*.
    Front flap devoted to blurb on *The Violent Bear It Away*;
    back flap advertises *A Voice Through a Cloud* and *Maiden
    Voyage*, both by Denton Welch.

Copies examined: DF; TxU; GB

Note: Published 30 June 1969 at 30s. 2500 copies were printed
    by Latimer Trend and Company. The text is from the same
    setting as the first edition, first American impression.
    All examined copies of this Faber and Faber issue have a
    cancel title page. In addition, George Bixby reports a
    copy purchased at the Strand Bookshop in New York with the
    dust jacket laminated over white boards, all covered with
    clear plastic. The outer edges are trimmed and speckled
    light red; the front flap is trimmed and pasted to the
    back free endpaper. This binding was apparently created
    for library use.
        Faber and Faber reissued *The Violent Bear It Away* in
    1980 with a new introduction by Paul Bailey, too late for
    inclusion in the bibliography.

                        II. SECOND EDITION

                    a. First Plating (American)

A3.II.a.1

First impression--New York: The New American Library, 1961

Title: The | VIOLENT | BEAR IT | AWAY | *by* Flannery O'Connor |
    "*From the days of John the Baptist* | *until now, the*

kingdom of heaven | *suffereth violence, and the violent* |
bear it away." | Matthew 11:12 | [*publisher's device*] | A
SIGNET BOOK | Published by THE NEW AMERICAN LIBRARY

Copyright notice: For Edward Francis O'Connor | 1896-1941 |
COPYRIGHT © 1955, 1960 BY FLANNERY O'CONNOR | All rights
reserved. No part of this book | may be reproduced
without permission. For | information address Farrar,
Straus & Cudahy, Inc., | 19 Union Square West, New York 3,
New York. | *Published as a SIGNET BOOK* | *By Arrangement
with Farrar, Straus & Cudahy, Inc.* | FIRST PRINTING, JUNE,
1961 | SIGNET TRADEMARK REG. U.S. PAT. OFF. AND FOREIGN
COUNTRIES | REGISTERED TRADEMARK--MARCA REGISTRADA | HECHO
EN CHICAGO, U.S.A. | *SIGNET BOOKS are published by* | *The
New American Library of World Literature, Inc.* | *501
Madison Avenue, New York 22, New York* | PRINTED IN THE
UNITED STATES OF AMERICA

Collation: 181 x 106.5 mm.; perfect binding, 80 leaves; pp.
[1-6] 7-160.

Contents: [1], blurb for *The Violent Bear It Away* and note on
reprint status; [2], advertisements, including one for
A Good Man Is Hard to Find; [3], title page; [4], copyright
notice; [5], section contents: PART I: 7 | II: 69 | III:
137; [6], blank; 7, text, continuing to 160 with same
chapter divisions as in first edition.

Typography and paper: Pagination centered 1.5 mm. below text
(p. 55). Running heads in cap and lower case italic,
spelled out, e.g., *Chapter One*, 7.5 mm. above first line
of text (p. 7). Text--40 lines 157.5 x 88.5 mm. (p. 55).
Paper--white wove; bulk 11 mm.

Binding: Stiff white paper wrappers. Printed on front: [*to
right*] D1937 | [*publisher's device with price of 50¢*] |
[*to left*] A novel of power and imagination by the author
of | A GOOD MAN IS HARD TO FIND..."Her talent for | fiction
is so great as to be almost overwhelming." | --Orville
Prescott, N.Y. TIMES | [*in purple (258)*] FLANNERY
O'CONNOR | [*in black*] THE VIOLENT BEAR | IT AWAY | [*boy
in hat running through a corn field, in shades of purple,
brown, and black, beneath an orange (36) sun*] | [*vertical
to left of illustration*] A SIGNET BOOK ... COMPLETE AND
UNABRIDGED; on spine: [*horizontal*] D | 1937 | [*vertical*]
THE VIOLENT BEAR IT AWAY Flannery O'Connor; back printed in
pink, purple, and black with blurbs for *The Violent Bear
It Away*, including a statement by Granville Hicks, as well
as biographical note and photograph of the author. All
edges trimmed and stained red (12).

Copies examined: GB; DF; GM

Note: Published in June 1961 at 50¢.   174,814 copies were
    printed.

II. SECOND EDITION

b. Second Plating (English)

A3.II.b.1

First impression--London: The New English Library, 1965

Title: The Violent | *Bear it Away* | Flannery O'Connor | 'From
    the days of John the Baptist until now, | The Kingdom of
    Heaven suffereth violence and | the violent bear it away.'
    <u>MATTHEW</u> 11 : 12. | [*publisher's device*] | A FOUR SQUARE
    BOOK

Copyright notice: For Edward Francis O'Connor | 1896-1941 |
    First published in Great Britain by Longmans, Green and
    Co. Ltd. in 1960. | Copyright © 1955, 1960 by Flannery
    O'Connor | [*asterisk*] | FIRST FOUR SQUARE EDITION October
    1965 | *Four Square Books are published by The New English
    Library Limited from Barnard's* | *Inn, Holborn, London
    E.C.1. Made and printed in Great Britain by Hunt Barnard
    & Co.* | *Limited, The Sign of the Dolphin, Aylesbury,
    Buckinghamshire*

Collation: 180 x 108 mm.; perfect binding, 80 leaves; pagina-
    tion same as in A3.II.a.1.

Contents: [1], half-title: THE VIOLENT | BEAR IT AWAY; [2],
    blank; [3], title page; [4], copyright notice; [5], text,
    continuing to 160 as in first American impression of this
    edition.

Typography and paper: Pagination same as in A3.II.a.1.   Text--
    40 lines 161.5 x 88 mm. (p. 55). Paper--white wove;
    bulk 9.5 mm.

Binding: Stiff white paper wrappers. Printed on front:
    [*publisher's device*] A FOUR SQUARE BOOK 3'6 | [*rule, with
    intersecting vertical rule dividing red from pink
    printing*] | [*in red (36)*] Flannery | O'Connor | *A vivid,
    obsessive* | *novel of depravity* | *in the Deep South* | [*in*

pink (255)] THE | VIOLENT | BEAR | IT AWAY | *[illustration
in tones of blue, tan, brown, pink, and green of man
standing in foreground with rifle and hat in hand, a boy
in middle ground sitting against a wagon wheel, and a
shack in background with wagon and fence behind it]*; on
spine: *[horizontal, publisher's device]* | 1338 | *[vertical,
in white on pink background]* THE VIOLENT BEAR IT AWAY *[in
black]* Flannery O'Connor; on back, printed in black, white,
pink, and red are quotations about the author from the *TLS*
and the *New Statesman*. All edges trimmed.

Copies examined: GB; DF; GM

Note: Published 7 October 1965 at 3/6d. 10,000 copies were
printed by Hunt Barnard & Company, Aylesbury.

THIRD EDITION

(*see* A4.I.a.1)

A4. THREE BY FLANNERY O'CONNOR

I. FIRST EDITION

a. First Plating (American)

A4.I.a.1

First impression--New York: The New American Library, 1964

Title: THREE | *[rule]* | Wise Blood | A Good Man Is Hard to
Find | The Violent Bear It Away | *[rule]* | FLANNERY
O'CONNOR | *[publisher's device]* | A SIGNET BOOK | Published
by The New American Library

Copyright notice: Wise Blood | Copyright © 1949, 1952, 1962
by Flannery O'Connor | A Good Man Is Hard to Find |
© Copyright, 1953, 1954, 1955, by Flannery O'Connor | The
Violent Bear It Away | Copyright © 1955, 1960 by Flannery
O'Connor | All rights reserved, including the right to
reproduce | this book, or portions thereof, in any form. |
Published as a SIGNET BOOK | *by arrangement with Farrar,*

Straus and Company, Inc., | *and Harcourt, Brace & World,*
Inc., | *who have authorized this softcover edition.* |
Hardcover editions of Wise Blood *and* The Violent Bear It |
Away *are available from Farrar, Straus and Company, Inc.;*
a hardcover edition of A Good Man Is Hard to Find | *is*
available from Harcourt, Brace & World, Inc. | First
printing, September, 1964 | SIGNET TRADEMARK REG. U.S. PAT.
OFF. AND FOREIGN COUNTRIES | REGISTERED TRADEMARK--MARCA
REGISTRADA | HECHO EN CHICAGO, U.S.A. | *SIGNET BOOKS are*
published by | *The New American Library of World Literature,*
Inc. | *501 Madison Avenue, New York, New York 10022* |
PRINTED IN THE UNITED STATES OF AMERICA

Collation: 180.5 x 107 mm.; perfect binding, 224 leaves;
pp. [1-8] 9-126 [127-128] 129-299 [300-304] 305-359 [360-
362] 363-423 [424-426] 427-447 [448].

Contents: [1], blurb on contents of book; [2], advertisements
for *Ship of Fools*, *The Voice at the Back Door*, *The Group*,
and *The Hard Blue Sky*; [3], title page; [4], copyright
notice; [5], table of contents; [6], blank; [7], fly-title
and dedication: WISE BLOOD | *for Regina*; [8], author's
note to the 1962 Farrar, Straus & Cudahy printing; 9-126,
text of *Wise Blood* with chapter headings on 9, 20,
24, 40, 46, 59, 66, 72, 80, 90, 94, 104, 109, and 116;
[127], fly-title and dedication: A GOOD MAN | IS HARD TO
FIND | *for Sally and Robert Fitzgerald*; [128]: THE DRAGON
IS BY THE SIDE OF THE ROAD, WATCHING | THOSE WHO PASS.
BEWARE LEST HE DEVOUR YOU. WE | GO TO THE FATHER OF SOULS,
BUT IT IS NECESSARY TO | PASS BY THE DRAGON. | St. Cyril
of Jerusalem; 129-299, text of *A Good Man Is Hard to Find*
with stories in same order as first edition beginning on
129, 144, 160, 171, 183, 195, 215, 233, 243, 262; [300],
blank; [301], fly-title and dedication: THE VIOLENT |
BEAR IT AWAY | *for Edward Francis O'Connor* | *1896-1941*;
[302]: "FROM THE DAYS OF JOHN THE BAPTIST UNTIL NOW, |
THE KINGDOM OF HEAVEN SUFFERETH VIOLENCE, AND | THE
VIOLENT BEAR IT AWAY." | *Matthew 11:12*; [303], divisional
half-title: PART | 1; [304], blank; 305-447, text with
divisional half-titles for parts 2 and 3 on 361 and 425,
each preceded and followed by a blank page, with chapters
beginning on 305, 335, 354, 363, 376, 387, 393, 398, 409,
427, 434, and 443; [448], advertisements for books by
Capote, Porter, McCarthy, Styron, Warren, and Baldwin.

Typography and paper: Pagination 5 mm. above text flush with
outer margins (p. 136) except at beginnings of chapters
or new stories where it is centered 1 mm. below last line

on page (p. 233). Running head, FLANNERY O'CONNOR, in all
caps Roman on all text versos except when they contain
beginning of a new story or chapter. Running heads, WISE
BLOOD and THE VIOLENT BEAR IT AWAY, in all caps Roman on
their respective text rectos except when they contain
beginning of a new chapter. Running heads (titles of
stories in *A Good Man Is Hard to Find*) in all caps Roman
on their respective text rectos except when they contain
beginning of a new story. Chapter and story titles in
all caps italic on first page of each new text section.
Text--47 lines 156.5 x 88.5 mm. (p. 150). Paper--white
wove; bulk 20 mm.

Binding: Stiff white paper wrappers. Printed on front: [*to
    left*] Q2524 [*to right, publisher's device with price of
    95¢*] | [*in red-orange (36)*] 3 [*in black*] by | FLANNERY |
    O'CONNOR | [*in red (11)*] Now complete and unabridged in
    one volume: | [*drawing of Model T Ford with man driving
    and woman with bare feet hanging over the door, a sign on
    the front in red*] CHURCH | WITHOUT | CHRIST | [*below car
    in black*] WISE | BLOOD | [*in pink (3)*] A GOOD | MAN IS |
    HARD TO | FIND | [*in blue (197)*] THE | VIOLENT | BEAR IT |
    AWAY | [*in black*] A SIGNET BOOK; on spine [*in white on
    black band at top, publisher's device*] | [*in black on
    white*] Q | 2524 | [*vertical*] THREE BY FLANNERY O'CONNOR;
    on back in red, black, blue, pink, and purple are blurbs,
    including quotations from William Goyen and Orville Pres-
    cott, and a biographical note on the author. All edges
    trimmed and stained red (12).

Copies examined: GB; DF; GM; TxU

Note: Published in April 1964 at 95¢ (according to information
    from the publisher), although the verso of the title page
    gives "September" as the month of the first impression.
    109,000 copies were printed. The New American Library
    also states that in April 1964 a 2nd impression of 5412
    copies was published for Canadian distribution. Subsequent
    reprints include a 3rd impression of 64,675 copies in
    October 1966, a 4th impression of 31,975 copies in November
    1967, a 5th impression of 31,965 copies in January 1969,
    a 6th impression of 50,420 copies in October 1969, a 7th
    impression of 47,570 copies in March 1971, and an 8th im-
    pression of 60,000 copies in March 1972. Beginning with
    the 7th impression, the price rose to $1.25. Through
    March of 1972 401,017 copies of *Three by Flannery O'Connor*
    were published. Advertisements on pp. [2] and [448] change
    in later impressions while the biographical note on the

back cover remains the same, not taking into account
Flannery O'Connor's death in 1964.

This book marks the fourth separate edition of *Wise
Blood* and third separate editions of *A Good Man Is Hard
to Find* and *The Violent Bear It Away*. The quotation on
p. [128] from St. Cyril of Jerusalem is the first appearance of this religious text in conjunction with *A
Good Man Is Hard to Find*.

A5. EVERYTHING THAT RISES MUST CONVERGE

I. FIRST EDITION

a. First Plating (American)

A5.I.a.1

First impression--New York: Farrar, Straus and Giroux, 1965

Title: Everything | That Rises | Must Converge | [*rule
tapered to point at right*] | *Flannery O'Connor* | Farrar,
Straus and Giroux | NEW YORK

Copyright notice: Copyright © 1956, 1957, 1958, 1960, 1961 |
1962, 1964, 1965 by the Estate of Mary Flannery O'Connor |
All rights reserved | Library of Congress catalog card
number: 65-13726 | First printing, 1965 | Acknowledgement
is made to the editors of the following publications | in
whose pages some of these stories first appeared: *The
Kenyon Re-* | *view, The Sewanee Review, New World Writing,
Partisan Review,* | *Esquire*, and *Harper's Bazaar*.

Collation: 202 x 135 mm.; [1-8]^{16} [9]^8 [10]^{16}, 152 leaves;
pp. [i-vi] vii-xxxiv [1-2] 3-269 [270]. Plate between
pp. [ii] and [iii].

Contents: [i], half-title: Everything That Rises Must Converge;
[ii]: *Books by Flannery O'Connor* | [*rule tapered to point
at left*] | WISE BLOOD | A GOOD MAN IS HARD TO FIND | THE
VIOLENT BEAR IT AWAY | EVERYTHING THAT RISES MUST CONVERGE;
plate tipped in, with photograph of Flannery O'Connor by
De Casseres on verso; [iii], title page; [iv], copyright
notice; [v], table of contents; [vi], blank; vii-xxxiv,
"Introduction" by Robert Fitzgerald; [1], divisional fly-

title: Everything That Rises Must Converge; [2], blank;
3, text, continuing to 269; [270], blank.

3-23 "Everything That Rises Must Converge" first appeared in *New World Writing*, No. 19, New York: The New
American Library, 1961. Pp. 74-90. [C.1961.10]
24-53 "Greenleaf" first appeared in *The Kenyon Review*,
18, No. 3 (Summer 1956), 384-410. [C.1956.6]
54-81 "A View of the Woods" first appeared in *Partisan
Review*, 24, No. 4 (Fall 1957), 475-496. [C.1957.5]
82-114 "The Enduring Chill" first appeared in *Harper's
Bazaar*, 91 (July 1958), 44-45, 94, 96, 100-102, 108.
[C.1958.4]
115-142 "The Comforts of Home" first appeared in *The
Kenyon Review*, 22 (Fall 1960), 523-554. [C.1960.3]
143-190 "The Lame Shall Enter First" first appeared in
The Sewanee Review, 70, No. 3 (Summer 1962), 337-379.
[C.1962.10]
191-218 "Revelation" first appeared in *The Sewanee
Review*, 72 (Spring 1964), 178-202. [C.1964.4]
219-244 "Parker's Back" first appeared in *Esquire*, 63,
No. 4 (April 1965), 76-78, 151-152, 154-155. [C.1965.3]
245-269 "Judgement Day" first appears in this collection.

Typography and paper: Pagination 6.5 mm. below text, in
square brackets near outer margins of type page (p. 149).
Running head in cap and lower case italic on rectos only;
changes with each story. Story title at beginning of
each new story in cap and lower case Roman beneath which
is a rule tapered to a point at right. Text--33 lines
150.5 x 94.5 mm. (p. 175). Paper--white wove; bulk 22 mm.

Binding: Blue (201) half-cloth with light blue (181) paper
boards. Printed on spine in white: Every- | thing |
That | Rises | Must | Converge | [*in blue (178), rule
tapered to a point at right*] | [*in white*] Flannery |
O'Connor | FARRAR | STRAUS AND | GIROUX. All edges
trimmed, top edges stained grey (191-186). Endpapers
grey (264-265).

Dust jacket: White printed in blue (178), green (129), grey
(265-266), and black. Printed on front: [*in blue, orna-
mental letters*] Flannery | O'Connor | [*in green, screened,
sans serif letters*] EVERY | [*in green, solid color*] THING |
[*in blue, screened*] THAT | [*in blue, solid color*] RISES |
[*in grey, screened*] MUST | [*in solid black*] CONVERGE; on
spine, all vertical: [*in green*] Farrar, Straus and
Giroux | [*in black, same ornamental letters as on cover*]

Flannery O'Connor | [*in blue, sans serif type*] EVERYTHING
THAT RISES MUST CONVERGE; on back author's name and dates
in blue, quotation from Thomas Merton about Flannery
O'Connor in black. Blurb on front and back flap.

Copies examined: GB; DF; GM; TxU

Note: Published 24 April 1965 at $4.95. Subsequent impressions
of both the hardback and its identical Noonday paperback
(N 287) have been numerous, but the information on the
verso of title pages in later impressions is somewhat
confusing when accumulated. Evidently, the true seventh
impression of the hardback in March 1968 was mistakenly
designated as the sixth. Also, sheets from the hardback have
been used for the Noonday paperback issue, with "Farrar,
Straus & Giroux" appearing on the title page while other
paperbacks are identified by "Noonday Press" on the title
page. Furthermore, some impressions of the paperback do
not carry the frontispiece photograph of Flannery O'Connor.
The following tabular account discloses some of the
anomalies, particularly involving the sixth through eighth
impressions from 1966 to 1969. There have also been a
Literary Guild Book Club impression released on 15 August
1965 and a Thomas More Book Club impression of 3000 copies
released in May 1965 at $4.95.

[hardbound edition]

Impression*			published price
1st	April	1965	4.95
2nd	May	1965	"
3rd	June	1965	"
4th	August	1965	"
5th	January	1966	"
6th	August	1966	"
6th	March	1968	5.50
7th	September	1968	"

[Noonday paperback]

1st	January	1966	1.95
2nd	March	1966	"
3rd	April	1966	"
4th	August	1966	"
5th	December	1966	"
6th FSG**	December	1966	"
6th	April	1967	"
6th FSG**	[March]	1968	"
7th	March	1968	"

8th	August	1969	"
9th FSG**	February	1970	"
10th FSG**	March	1971	"
11th	April	1972	"
12th	April	1973	"

   * The number of the impression and the year are listed
     as they appear on the versos of the title pages.
  ** Farrar, Straus & Giroux is the only imprint on the
     title page.

I. FIRST EDITION

b. Second Plating (English)

A5.I.b.1

First impression--London: Faber and Faber, 1966

Title: Everything | That Rises | Must Converge | [*rule tapered
   to point at right*] | *Flannery O'Connor* | Faber and Faber |
   24 Russell Square London

Copyright notice: First published in England mcmlxvi | *by
   Faber and Faber Limited* | *24 Russell Square London WC1* |
   Printed in Great Britain by* | *Latimer Trend & Co Ltd
   Whitstable* | *All rights reserved* | Acknowledgement is
   made to the editors of the following publi- | cations in
   whose pages some of these stories first appeared: *The* |
   *Kenyon Review, The Sewanee Review, New World Writing,
   Partisan* | *Review, Esquire,* and *Harper's Bazaar.* |
   Copyright © 1956, 1957, 1958, 1960, 1961 | 1962, 1964,
   1965 by the Estate of Mary Flannery O'Connor

Collation: 199 x 130 mm.; $[1-17]^8$ $[18]^4$, 140 leaves; pp. [i-
   vi] [1-2] 3-269 [270-274].

Contents: [i], half-title: Everything That Rises Must Converge;
   [ii], blank; [iii], title page; [iv], copyright notice;
   [v], table of contents same as American impression, except lacking "Introduction"; [vi], blank; [1], biographical
   note of 23 lines headed by author's name (text similar to
   that on back flap of dust jacket); [2], blank; 3, text,
   continuing as in A5.I.a.1 to 269; [270-274], blank.

Typography and paper: Pagination and text same as in American
   impression. Paper--white wove; bulk 18.5 mm.

Binding: Bluish green (164) cloth boards. Spine stamped in
    gold: Everything | That Rises | Must | Converge |
    [*bullet*] | Flannery | O'Connor | FABER. All edges
    trimmed. Endpapers white.

Dust jacket: White printed in black and bluish green. Printed
    on front: [*vertical, each word in black and two shades of*
    bluish green, three images of each word overlapping]
    Everything | That | Rises | Must | Converge | [*horizontal,*
    in the lighter of above shades of bluish green] FLANNERY |
    O'CONNOR; printed on spine: [*in black*] Every- | thing |
    That | Rises | Must | Converge | [*in darker bluish green*]
    by | *Flannery* | *O'Connor* | [*vertical, in lighter bluish*
    green] FLANNERY | O'CONNOR | [*horizontal, in darker bluish*
    green] FABER; printed on back in black are advertisements
    for books by Jim Hunter, Eugene Ionesco, Denton Welch,
    and John McGahern; one bluish green rule. Front flap
    contains blurb on *Everything That Rises Must Converge*;
    back flap presents same biographical sketch as found on
    p. [1].

Copies examined: GB; DF; GM; TxU

Note: Published 24 March 1966 at 25s. 2470 copies were
    printed. While the text is from the same setting as the
    Farrar, Straus and Giroux American impression, the major
    difference between the English and American impressions
    is that this book does not have Robert Fitzgerald's in-
    troduction. One copy has been examined with a variant
    title page containing an extra line of type--FABER AND
    FABER--in all caps Roman just above the last two lines of
    type on the page.
        Faber and Faber reissued *Everything That Rises Must*
    Converge in 1980 with a new introduction by Hermione Lee,
    too late for inclusion in the bibliography.

                           II. SECOND EDITION

                      a. First Plating (American)

A5.II.a.1

First impression--New York: The New American Library, 1967

Title: Flannery O'Connor | [*decorative rule*] | EVERYTHING |
    THAT RISES | MUST CONVERGE | [*publisher's device*] | A
    SIGNET BOOK | Published by | The New American Library

Copyright notice: COPYRIGHT © 1956, 1957, 1958, 1960, 1961,
   1962, 1964, 1965 | BY THE ESTATE OF MARY FLANNERY
   O'CONNOR | All rights reserved. For information, address
   Farrar, Straus and | Giroux, Inc., 19 Union Square West,
   New York, | New York 10003. | FIRST PRINTING, JUNE, 1967 |
   Acknowledgment is made to the editors of the following |
   publications in whose pages some of these stories first
   appeared: | *The Kenyon Review, The Sewanee Review, New
   World Writing,* | *Partisan Review, Esquire,* and *Harper's
   Bazaar.* | SIGNET TRADEMARK REG. U.S. PAT. OFF. AND FOREIGN
   COUNTRIES | REGISTERED TRADEMARK--MARCA REGISTRADA | HECHO
   EN CHICAGO, U.S.A. | *SIGNET BOOKS are published by* | *The
   New American Library, Inc.,* | *1301 Avenue of the Americas,
   New York, New York 10019* | PRINTED IN THE UNITED STATES OF
   AMERICA

Collation: 178 x 108 mm.; perfect binding, 112 leaves; pp. [i-
   vi] vii-xxvii [28] 29-43 [44] 45-165 [166] 167-205 [206]
   207-224.

Contents: [i], blurbs on *Everything That Rises Must Converge*
   from the *New York Herald Tribune, Time,* and *The National
   Review* and a biographical note on the author; [ii], Signet
   advertisements; [iii], title page; [iv], copyright notice;
   [v], contents page; [vi], blank; vii-xxvii, "Introduction";
   [28], blank; 29, text, continuing to 224 in same order as
   in first edition.

Typography and paper: Pagination 3 mm. (p. 164) above type,
   flush with outer margins; centered 1 mm. (p. 45) below
   last line on pages opening a new story. Text--44 lines
   151 x 89 mm. (p. 70). Paper--white wove; bulk 15 mm.

Binding: Stiff white paper wrappers. Printed on front: [*in
   red (ll) to right of first three lines*] T3177 | [*Signet
   price imprint 75¢*] | [*beginning flush left*] "The best
   collection of shorter | fiction published in America
   during the past | twenty years."--Theodore Solotaroff,
   Book Week | [*in black*] Flannery O'Connor | A *Book Week*
   panel of 200 writers and critics judged | her work among
   "the most distinguished fiction | published in America
   during the years 1945-1965." | Everything That Rises |
   Must Converge | [*drawing of bus with woman and man looking
   out the windows in tones of red and brown*] | [*reversed in
   white near base*] A Signet Book | complete and unabridged;
   on spine: [*red square at top with publisher's device
   printed in black*] | [*on white background in red*] T | 3177 |
   [*reading down*] Everything That Rises Must Converge [*in*

black] Flannery O'Connor; back contains blurbs on *Every-thing That Rises Must Converge* by Webster Schott, Lillian Smith, and Francis King. All edges trimmed, stained red (12).

Copies examined: GB; DF; GM; TxU

Note: Published June 1967 at 75¢. 101,995 copies were issued in the United States while a 2nd impression of 8335 copies was issued in Canada. A 3rd impression of 27,390 copies was published in June 1969; a 4th impression of 27,395 copies was published in April 1971. The 4th impression was priced at 95¢ rather than 75¢. Signet advertisements on p. [ii] change in later impressions along with the design on the spine.

A6. MYSTERY AND MANNERS

I. FIRST EDITION

a. First Plating (American)

A6.I.a.1

First impression--New York: Farrar, Straus and Giroux, 1969

Title: Flannery O'Connor | *[rule]* | MYSTERY AND | MANNERS | *[swelled rule]* | *Occasional Prose, selected & edited by* | *Sally and Robert Fitzgerald* | *[device of 8 pyramids with periods, a rule, three abstract fish, a thick rule]* | Farrar, Straus & Giroux | NEW YORK

Copyright notice: Copyright © *1957, 1961, 1963, 1964, 1966, 1967, 1969* | *by the Estate of Mary Flannery O'Connor* | *Copyright* © *1962 by Flannery O'Connor* | *Copyright* © *1961 by Farrar, Straus and Cudahy, Inc.* | *All rights reserved* | *First printing, 1969* | *Library of Congress catalog card number: 69-15409* | *Published simultaneously in Canada by* | *Doubleday Canada Ltd., Toronto* | *Printed in the United States of America* | *Design by Guy Fleming*

Collation: 209 x 143 mm.; [1-8]^{16}, 128 leaves; pp. [a-b] [i-iv] v-ix [x] [1-2] 3-21 [22-24] 25-59 [60-62] 63-118

[119-120] 121-140 [141-142] 143-209 [210-212] 213-228
[229-230] 231-237 [238-244].

Contents: [a], blank; [b]: *Books by* FLANNERY O'CONNOR |
[*rule*] | *Wise Blood* | *A Good Man Is Hard to Find* | *The
Violent Bear It Away* | *Everything That Rises Must
Converge* | *Mystery and Manners;* [i], half-title: MYSTERY
& MANNERS; [ii], blank; [iii], title page; [iv], copyright
notice; v-vi, contents; vii-ix, [x], Foreword; [1], divisional half-title: I; [2], blank; 3-21, text; [22], blank;
[23], divisional half-title: II; [24], blank; 25-59, text;
[60], blank; [61], divisional half-title: III; [62],
blank; 63-118, text; [119], divisional half-title: IV;
[120], blank; 121-140, text; [141], divisional half-title:
V; [142], blank; 143-209, text; [210], blank; [211],
divisional half-title: VI; [212], blank; 213-228, text;
[229]: APPENDIX & NOTES; [230], blank; 231-237, text;
[238-244], blank.

3-21   "The King of the Birds" first appeared as "Living
with a Peacock" in *Holiday*, 30, No. 3 (September 1961),
52, 110-112, 114.   [C.1961.16]
25-35   "The Fiction Writer & His Country" first appeared
in *The Living Novel* [B6]; excerpts in *The Added Dimension*
[B14].
36-50   "Some Aspects of the Grotesque in Southern Fiction"
first appeared in the *Cluster Review*, Seventh Issue
(March 1965), 5-6, 22.   [C.1965.2]
51-59   "The Regional Writer" first appeared in *Esprit*, 7,
No. 1 (Winter, 1963), 31-35.   [C.1963.15]
63-86   "The Nature and Aim of Fiction" first appears in
this collection.
87-106   "Writing Short Stories" first appears in this
collection.
107-114   "On Her Own Work: A Reasonable Use of the Un-
reasonable" first appears in this collection.
114-115   "On Her Own Work: The Mystery of Freedom" first
appeared as the introductory note for the second impression of the first edition of *Wise Blood*.   [A1.I.a.2]
115-118   "On Her Own Work: In the Devil's Territory": a
portion of this appeared as "The Novelist and Free Will"
in *Fresco*, 1, No. 2 (Winter 1961), 100-101.   [C.1961.5]
121-134   "The Teaching of Literature" first appears in
this collection.
135-140   "Total Effect and the Eighth Grade" first appeared as "Fiction Is a Subject with a History: It
Should Be Taught That Way" in *The Georgia Bulletin* (21
March 1963), 1.   [C.1963.4]

143-153 "The Church and the Fiction Writer" first appeared in *America* (30 March 1957), 733-735. [C.1957.3]
154-168 "Novelist and Believer" first appears in this
collection.
169-190 "Catholic Novelists and Their Readers" first
appeared in a much different version as "The Role of
the Catholic Novelist" in *Greyfriar, Siena Studies in
Literature*, 7 (1964), 5-12. [C.1964.5]
191-209 "The Catholic Novelist in the Protestant South"
first appeared in a different version in *Viewpoint*
(Spring 1966). [C.1966.1]
213-228 "Introduction to *A Memoir of Mary Ann*" first
appeared in *A Memoir of Mary Ann*. [B11]
232-233 ["Review of *The Presence of Grace* by J.F. Powers"]
first appeared in *The Bulletin* (31 March 1956).
[C.1956.1]
233-234 [Extract from "Flannery O'Connor / An Interview"]
first appeared in *Jubilee*, 11, No. 2 (June 1963), 33-35.
[C.1963.7]

Typography and paper: Pagination in italic numerals with one
square bracket on gutter side of each number, 4.5 mm.
(p. 45) below text, 12 mm. from inner margin of each type
page. Bracket omitted when numeral is centered 5 mm.
below last line on opening page of each new contribution.
Running head, FLANNERY O'CONNOR, in caps and small caps
on all text versos except in Foreword, Appendix, and Notes
which have their own generic running heads. Running heads
in cap and lower case italic on all text rectos except
when a new chapter begins on a recto. Text--27 lines
152 x 88.5 mm. (p. 214). Paper--white wove; bulk 18 mm.

Binding: Half-cloth with yellow-green (130-131) paper boards.
Blue (177-178) cloth spine stamped: [*in gold, device of
6 pyramids with periods at base*] | [*thick rule*] | [*in
silver*] *Flannery* | *O'Connor* | [*in gold, thick rule*] |
[*pyramid device, periods at top*] | [*pyramid device,
periods at bottom*] | [*thick rule*] | [*in silver*] *Mystery* |
& | *Manners* | [*in gold, thick rule*] | [*pyramid device,
periods at top*] | [*pyramid device, periods at bottom*] |
[*thick rule*] | [*in silver*] FARRAR | STRAUS | GIROUX | [*in
gold, thick rule*] | [*pyramid device, periods at top*].
Top and bottom edges trimmed, top edge stained yellowish
pink (27). Endpapers yellow (83-82).

Dust jacket: Designed by Guy Fleming; white, front printed
with full-color photograph of a peacock overprinted with
author, title, and editor in white and yellow (83) in a

black panel. On back of the dust jacket is a black-and-white photograph of Miss O'Connor on steps of her home with a peacock; yellow panels above and below photo, printing in black on lower panel.

Copies examined: GB; DF; GM; TxU

Note: Published 12 May 1969 at $6.95. Noonday paperback #375 was published in December 1969 at $2.25, printed from the original setting. A second paperback impression was published in December 1970.

I. FIRST EDITION

b. Second Plating (English)

A6.I.b.1

First impression--London: Faber and Faber, 1972

Title: Flannery O'Connor | [*rule*] | MYSTERY AND | MANNERS | [*swelled rule*] | *Occasional Prose, selected & edited by* | *Sally and Robert Fitzgerald* | FABER AND FABER | 3 Queen Square | London

Copyright notice: First published in 1972 | *by Faber and Faber Limited* | *Printed in Great Britain by* | *John Dickens and Co Ltd, Northampton* | *All rights reserved* | *ISBN 0 571 09348 5* | *Copyright* © *1957, 1961, 1963, 1964, 1966, 1967, 1969* | *by the Estate of Mary Flannery O'Connor* | *Copyright* © *1962 by Flannery O'Connor* | *Copyright* © *1961 by Farrar, Straus and Cudahy, Inc.*

Collation: 196 x 126 mm.; [A]^8 B-O^8 P^4 Q^8, 124 leaves; pp. [i-iv] v-ix [x] [1-2] 3-237 [238].

Contents: [i], half-title; [ii], books by Flannery O'Connor, same as first American impression, except *Mystery and Manners* is omitted; [iii], title page; [iv], copyright notice; v-[x], [1]-237 same as first American impression; [238], blank.

Typography and paper: Pagination same as in first American impression except for omission of square brackets on gutter side of each numeral. Running heads same. Text--same as first American impression. Paper--white wove; bulk 16.5 mm.

Binding: Blue (185-186) cloth boards. Stamped in gold on spine, reading down: *MYSTERY &* | *MANNERS Flannery O'Connor* [*reading across*] FABER. All edges trimmed.

Dust jacket: White printed in black, blue (177), and grey green (150).

Copies examined: GB; DF; TxU

Note: Published 24 January 1972 at £2.50. 2000 copies were printed by John Dickens & Co. The book is found in two binding states:

(1) 1000 sets of sheets bound and stamped: *MYSTERY & S and* | *MANNERS R Fitzgerald* [*reading across*] FABER
(2) 1000 sets of sheets bound and stamped: *MYSTERY &* | *MANNERS Flannery O'Connor* [*reading across*] FABER.

A7. THE COMPLETE STORIES

I. FIRST EDITION

a. First Plating (American)

A7.I.a.1

First impression--New York: Farrar, Straus and Giroux, 1971

Title: Flannery O'Connor | [*swelled rule*] | THE | COMPLETE | STORIES | [*device of three abstract fish*] | *Farrar, Straus and Giroux* | NEW YORK

Copyright notice: Copyright © 1946, 1948, 1956, 1957, 1958, 1960, 1961, 1962, | 1963, 1964, 1965, 1970, 1971 by the Estate of Mary Flannery | O'Connor. Copyright © 1949, 1952, 1955, 1960, 1962 by | Flannery O'Connor. Introduction copyright © 1971 by Robert | Giroux; quotations from letters are used by permission of | Robert Fitzgerald and of the Estate and are copyright © 1971 | by the Estate of Mary Flannery O'Connor. The ten stories | from *A Good Man Is Hard to Find,* copyright © 1953, 1954, | 1955 by Flannery O'Connor, are used by special arrangement | with Harcourt Brace Jovanovich, Inc. | All rights reserved | First printing, 1971 | Library of Congress catalog card number:

72-171492 | ISBN 0-374-12752-2 | Published simultaneously
in Canada | by Doubleday Canada Ltd., Toronto | Printed
in the United States of America | DESIGNED BY HERB JOHNSON

Collation: 121.5 x 142 mm.; [1-18]^{16}, 288 leaves; pp. [a-b]
[i-iv] v-xvii [xviii] [1-2] 3-555 [556].

Contents: [a-b], blank; [i], half-title: THE COMPLETE STORIES
OF | Flannery O'Connor; [ii]: *by Flannery O'Connor* | *Wise*
Blood, NOVEL | *A Good Man Is Hard to Find*, STORIES | *The*
Violent Bear It Away, NOVEL | *Everything That Rises Must*
Converge, STORIES | *Mystery and Manners*, ESSAYS EDITED
BY | SALLY AND ROBERT FITZGERALD; [iii], title page; [iv],
copyright notice; v-vi, contents; vii-xvii, Introduction;
[xviii], blank; [1], fly-title; [2], blank; 3-550, text;
551-555, Notes; [556], blank.

3-14 "The Geranium" first appeared in *Accent*, 6 (Summer
    1946), 245-253. [C.1946.1]
15-25 "The Barber" first appeared in *New Signatures 1948*,
    113-124. [B1]
26-32 "Wildcat" first appeared in *The North American Re-*
    view, 255, No. 1 (Spring 1970). [C.1970.1]
33-41 "The Crop" first appeared in *Mademoiselle*, 72,
    No. 6 (April 1971). [C.1971.1]
42-53 "The Turkey" first appeared as "The Capture" in
    Mademoiselle, 28 (November 1948), 148-149, 195-196,
    198-201. [C.1948.2]
54-62 "The Train" first appeared in *The Sewanee Review*,
    56, No. 2 (April-June 1948), 261-271. [C.1948.1]
63-80 "The Peeler" first appeared in *Partisan Review*,
    16, No. 12 (December 1949), 1189-1206. [C.1949.3]
81-94 "The Heart of the Park" first appeared in *Partisan*
    Review, 16, No. 2 (February 1949), 138-151. [C.1949.1]
95-107 "A Stroke of Good Fortune" first appeared as "The
    Woman on the Stairs" in *Tomorrow*, 8, No. 12 (August
    1949), 40-44. [C.1949.2]
108-116 "Enoch and the Gorilla" first appeared in *New*
    World Writing, No. 1 (April 1952), 67-74. [C.1952.1]
117-133 "A Good Man Is Hard to Find" first appeared in
    The Avon Book of Modern Writing, 186-199. [B2]
134-144 "A Late Encounter with the Enemy" first appeared
    in *Harper's Bazaar*, 87, No. 4 (September 1953), 234,
    247, 249, 252. [C.1953.3]
145-156 "The Life You Save May Be Your Own" first appeared
    in *The Kenyon Review*, 15, No. 2 (Spring 1953), 195-207.
    [C.1953.1]
157-174 "The River" first appeared in *The Sewanee Review*,
    61, No. 3 (Summer 1953), 455-475. [C.1953.2]

175-193 "A Circle in the Fire" first appeared in *The Kenyon Review*, 16, No. 2 (Spring 1954), 169-190. [C.1954.1]

194-235 "The Displaced Person" first appeared in *The Sewanee Review*, 62, No. 4 (Autumn 1954), 634-654. [C.1954.3]

236-248 "A Temple of the Holy Ghost" first appeared in *Harper's Bazaar*, 88, No. 5 (May 1954), 108-109, 162-164, 169. [C.1954.2]

249-270 "The Artificial Nigger" first appeared in *The Kenyon Review*, 17, No. 2 (Spring 1955), 169-192. [C.1955.1]

271-291 "Good Country People" first appeared in *Harper's Bazaar*, 89, No. 6 (June 1955), 64-65, 116-117, 121-122, 124, 130. [C.1955.2]

292-310 "You Can't Be Any Poorer Than Dead" first appeared in *New World Writing*, No. 8 (October 1955), 91-97. [C.1955.3]

311-334 "Greenleaf" first appeared in *The Kenyon Review*, No. 3 (Summer 1956), 384-410. [C.1956.6]

335-356 "A View of the Woods" first appeared in *Partisan Review*, 24, No. 4 (Fall 1957), 475-496. [C.1957.5]

357-382 "The Enduring Chill" first appeared in *Harper's Bazaar*, 91, No. 2960 (July 1958), 44-45, 94, 96, 100-102, 108. [C.1958.4]

383-404 "The Comforts of Home" first appeared in *The Kenyon Review*, 22, No. 4 (Autumn 1960), 523-554. [C.1960.3]

405-420 "Everything That Rises Must Converge" first appeared in *New World Writing*, No. 19 (1961), 74-90. [C.1961.10]

421-444 "The Partridge Festival" first appeared in *The Critic*, 19, No. 4 (February-March 1961), 20-23, 82-85. [C.1961.4]

445-482 "The Lame Shall Enter First" first appeared in *The Sewanee Review*, 70, No. 3 (Summer 1962), 337-379. [C.1962.10]

483-487 "Why Do the Heathen Rage?" first appeared in *Esquire*, 60, No. 1 (July 1963), 60-61. [C.1963.9]

488-509 "Revelation" first appeared in *The Sewanee Review*, 72, No. 2 (Spring 1964), 178-202. [C.1964.4]

510-530 "Parker's Back" first appeared in *Esquire*, 63, No. 4 (April 1965), 76-78, 151-152, 154-155. [C.1965.3]

531-550 "Judgement Day" first appears in this collection.

Typography and paper: Pagination 4 mm. (p. 303) above text flush with outer margins of type page; 3.5 mm. (p. 292) below text flush with outer margins on pages where a new

story begins. Running head *The Complete Stories of Flannery
O'Connor* preceded by a diagonal rule on all text versos
except when a new story begins on a verso. Running heads
(title of story) followed by a diagonal rule on all text
rectos except when a new story begins on a recto. Text—
38 lines 174.5 x 111.5 mm. (p. 473); some pages have 37
lines 170.5 x 111.5 mm. (p. 474). Paper—white wove;
bulk 37 mm.

Binding: Green (122-120) cloth boards. Spine stamped in gold:
    Flannery | O'Connor | [*swelled rule*] | The | Complete |
    Stories | FARRAR | STRAUS | GIROUX. Top and bottom edges
    trimmed, fore edges rough trimmed, top edges stained grey-
    red (19). Endpapers red (13-12).

Dust jacket: Designed by Charles Skaggs; white, printed mostly
    in black, greenish blue (169), and green (141).

Copies examined: GB; DF; TxU

Note: Published 8 November 1971 at $10.00. Subsequent im-
    pressions have been published as follows: second impression,
    January 1972; third impression, March 1972; fourth im-
    pression, August 1972; fifth impression, November 1972;
    sixth impression, March 1973. This book was also issued
    by Farrar, Straus & Giroux as a paperback in their new
    Sunburst series (S13) in August 1972 at $3.95. Subsequent
    paperback impressions were published in November 1972 and
    March 1973. The first Sunburst paperbacks of August 1972
    were manufactured from sheets for the fourth impression of
    the hardback.
       The Complete Stories was offered as a selection by the
    Saturday Review Book Club for release in April 1972.
    The binding and dust jacket are identical to the regular
    issue except that the fore edges are trimmed and the top
    edges are stained a lighter red (15). The Thomas More
    Book Club offered *Complete Stories* from sheets from the
    third impression for release in October 1972. The binding
    and dust jacket are the same as the regular issue.

A8.   THE HABIT OF BEING

I. FIRST EDITION

a. First Plating (American)

A8.I.a.1

First impression--New York: Farrar, Straus, Giroux, 1979

Title: FLANNERY O'CONNOR | *[swelled rule]* | *THE HABIT* | *OF*
    BEING | LETTERS EDITED AND | WITH AN INTRODUCTION | BY
    Sally Fitzgerald | *[leaf device]* | *Farrar • Straus •*
    Giroux | NEW YORK

Copyright notice: Copyright © 1979 by Regina O'Connor |
    Introduction copyright © 1979 by Sarah Fitzgerald | *All*
    rights reserved First printing, 1979 | *Printed in the*
    United States of America | *Published simultaneously in*
    Canada | *by McGraw-Hill Ryerson Ltd., Toronto* | *Designed*
    by Cynthia Krupat | *Library of Congress Cataloging in*
    Publication Data | *O'Connor, Flannery / The habit of*
    being | *Includes index* | *1. O'Connor, Flannery--*
    Correspondence | *2. Novelists, American--20th century--*
    Correspondence | *I. Fitzgerald, Sally / II. Title* |
    PS3565.C57Z48 1978 / 813'.5'4 [B] *78-11559*

Collation: 228 x 149 mm.; [1-20][16], *320 leaves; pp. [i-xi]*
    xii-xviii [xix-xxii] [1-2] 3-50 [51-52] 53-311 [312-314]
    315-555 [556-558] 559-596 [597-598] 599-617 [618].

Contents: [i], blank; [ii]: BOOKS BY | *Flannery O'Connor*
    [seven titles listed]; [iii], half-title: The Habit of
    Being; [iv], blank; [v], title page; [vi], copyright
    notice; *[vii], dedication: To Regina Cline O'Connor* | *in*
    gratitude for letting readers | *come to know her daughter*
    better; [viii], blank; [ix], contents page; [x], blank;
    [xi]-[xix], introduction; [xx], blank; [xxi-xxii],
    editor's note; *[1], divisional half-title: PART I* |
    [swelled rule] | *UP NORTH AND* | *GETTING HOME* | *1948-1952* |
    [leaf device]; [2], blank; 3-50, text; [51], divisional
    half-title: *PART II* | *[swelled rule]* | *DAY IN AND* | *DAY*
    OUT | *1953-1958 [leaf device]; [52], blank; 53-311, text;*
    [312], blank; [313], divisional half-title: PART III |
    [swelled rule] | *"THE VIOLENT* | *BEAR IT AWAY"* | *1959-*
    1963 | *[leaf device]; [314], blank; 315-555, text; [556],*
    blank; *[557], divisional half-title: PART IV* | *[swelled*

rule] | *THE LAST YEAR* | *1964* | [*leaf device*]; [558],
blank; 559-596, text; [597]: *INDEX*; [598], blank; 599-
617, index; [618], blank.

Typography and paper: Pagination 6 mm. below text near outer
   edges of each page (p. 361). Text--44 lines 187 x 105 mm.
   (p. 187). Paper--white wove; bulk 38.5 mm.

Binding: Black cloth boards. Spine stamped in gold and
   yellowish green (136): [*in gold*] [*rule*] | *Flannery* |
   O'Connor | [*in green, leaf device*] | [*in gold*] *The
   Habit* | *of Being* | [*in green, leaf device*] | [*in gold*]
   FSG | [*rule*]. Upper cover: [*in gold*] *Flannery O'Connor* |
   [*swelled rule*] | [*in green, leaf device*]. All edges
   trimmed, top edges stained yellow (104). Endpapers white.

Dust jacket: White printed in black, red-orange (34), and
   yellow (82-83) on front, a field of black: [*red*] LETTERS
   OF | [*white*] Flannery | O'Connor | [*red*] THE HABIT | OF
   BEING | SELECTED AND EDITED BY Sally Fitzgerald |
   [*stylized phoenix in white and black on field of yellow
   and red-orange flames*]; on spine, reading down: [*black*]
   Flannery O'Connor | [*red*] THE HABIT OF BEING | [*horizontal,
   in black*] FARRAR | STRAUS | GIROUX; on back is a photo-
   graph of the author by Joe McTyre captioned: FLANNERY
   O'CONNOR AND PEACOCK | ON THE PORCH OF HER HOME,
   "ANDALUSIA," | IN MILLEDGEVILLE, GEORGIA; blurb on flaps.
   Dust jacket designed by Janet Halverson.

Copy examined: DF

Note: Published 16 March 1979 at $15.00. In 1980 Random
   House issued *The Habit of Being* as a Vintage Books paperback (V-259) at $6.95. Faber and Faber issued *The Habit
   of Being* in 1980, too late for inclusion in the bibliography.

Section B
Contributions to Books

Title: NEW SIGNATURES I | A SELECTION OF COLLEGE WRITING |
    edited by | Alan Swallow | [*device*] | THE PRESS OF JAMES
    A. DECKER | Prairie City, Illinois

Collation: 195 x 131 mm. Pp. xiii, 178.

Contents: "The Barber," pp. 113-124. First publication.

Binding: Grey (near 265) cloth boards; stamped in gold down
    spine: *NEW SIGNATURES 1948* [*space*] DECKER; stamped in
    gold on front: [*decorative rule*] | NEW SIGNATURES 1948 |
    Edited *by* ALAN SWALLOW | [*decorative rule*]. Sheets are
    in gatherings but appear to be stabbed. All edges trimmed.

Note: Published in 1947. In addition to the difference be-
    tween the wording on the title page and the spine, the
    half-title reads *AMERICAN SIGNATURES.* Also, on the verso
    of the title page the book is copyrighted by Alan Swallow
    in 1947 rather than 1948, the date on the spine. A
    binding variant has been examined in blue-grey (203) cloth
    boards printed in blue (183) down spine: NEW SIGNATURES
    1948--SWALLOW; all edges trimmed. 197 x 136 mm. The
    sheets are in gatherings and stitched in normal fashion.
    "The Barber" was reprinted in *The Atlantic* [C.1970.?] and
    collected in *Complete Stories* [A7].

Title: [*on a double spread*] the avon book of | A collection of
    original contributions | by today's leading writers. |
    Robert Musil | Colette | Diana Trilling | Flannery
    O'Connor | Eleanor Clark | Patrick O'Brian | Irving Howe |
    Isaac Rosenfeld | and 13 others || MODERN | WRITING |
    edited by | William Phillips and Philip Rahv | [*head of
    Shakespeare*] | AVON PUBLICATIONS, INC. | 575 Madison
    Avenue New York 22, N.Y.

Collation: 180 x 107 mm.   Pp. 281.

Contents: "A Good Man Is Hard to Find," pp. 186-199.   First
    publication.

Binding: White paper wrappers printed in black, white, yellow
    (83), red (12-11), and pale blue (203); all edges trimmed
    and stained orange-yellow (71).

Note: Published 21 September 1953.   This story is collected
    in *A Good Man Is Hard to Find* [A2], *Three* [A4], and *Com-
    plete Stories* [A7].

B3   PRIZE STORIES   1954

Title: PRIZE STORIES 1954: *The O. Henry Awards* | *Selected
    and Edited by* | PAUL ENGLE *and* HANSFORD MARTIN | *Doubleday
    & Company, Inc., Garden City, N.Y.* 1954

Collation: 208 x 138 mm.   Pp. 316.

Contents: "The Life You Save May Be Your Own," pp. 194-204.

Binding: Black cloth boards printed on spine in yellow (82)
    and reddish orange (35).   All edges trimmed.   White dust
    jacket designed by Margot Tomes printed in black, blue
    (182), orange (50), and yellow (83-84).

Note: Published 21 January 1954.   First published in *The
    Kenyon Review* [C.1953.1], this story was collected in
    A Good Man Is Hard to Find [A2], *Three* [A4], and *Complete
    Stories* [A7].

B4   PRIZE STORIES   1955

Title: PRIZE STORIES 1955: *The O. Henry Awards* | *Selected and
    Edited by* | PAUL ENGLE *and* HANSFORD MARTIN | *Doubleday &
    Company, Inc., Garden City, N.Y., 1955*

Collation: 207 x 138 mm.   Pp. [ii], 313.

Contents: "A Circle in the Fire," pp. 35-52.

Binding: Black cloth boards printed on spine in orange (50)
    and light brown-grey (63).   All edges trimmed.   White

dust jacket designed by Margot Tomes, printed in black, brown (55-54), brilliant yellow (83), and pale green (149-144).

Note: Published 6 January 1955. This story was first pub-lished in *The Kenyon Review* [C.1954.1] and was a second-prize winner in the O. Henry Awards of 1955. It was re-printed in *The Best American Short Stories of 1955* in September 1955 and collected in *A Good Man Is Hard to Find* [A2], *Three* [A4], and *Complete Stories* [A7].

B5   THE BEST AMERICAN SHORT STORIES   1956

Title: THE | [*in red (11-13)*)] *Best* | [*in black*] AMERICAN | SHORT STORIES | 1956 | [*decorative rule*] | *and the Yearbook of the American Short Story* | [*rule*] | *Edited by* | MARTHA FOLEY | [*publisher's device*] | HOUGHTON MIFFLIN COMPANY • BOSTON | The Riverside Press Cambridge | 1956

Collation: 203 x 137 mm. Pp. [xiv], 368.

Contents: "The Artificial Nigger," pp. 264-284.

Binding: Light yellow brown (near 76) cloth boards printed in deep red-brown (44) on front and spine. Top and bottom edges trimmed; fore edges rough trimmed. White dust jacket with pictorial design by William Barss printed in black, deep red-orange (36-40 and 38), medium orange (50-53), medium blue-green (164-265), shades of light green (141), and pale reddish purple (244).

Note: Published 29 October 1956. A Ballantine paperback (#F204) edition of this book was published in March 1957 in a new setting; O'Connor's story appears on pp. 274-294 of the paperback. "The Artificial Nigger" was first published in *The Kenyon Review* [C.1955.1]; collected in *A Good Man Is Hard to Find* [A2], *Three* [A4], and *Complete Stories* [A7].

B6   THE LIVING NOVEL   1957

Title: [*on a double spread*] THE | LIVING || EDITED BY GRANVILLE HICKS | NOVEL: | a symposium | The Macmillan Company: New York: 1957

Collation: 208 x 138 mm.   Pp. [xvi], 230.

Contents: "The Fiction Writer and His Country," pp. 157-164.
   First publication.

Binding: Half-bound in pale blue (185) and dark blue-grey
   (192) patterned paper boards with dark blue (183-187)
   cloth spine printed in white.   All edges trimmed.   White
   dust jacket designed by Leo Manso printed in medium blue
   (182-186) and light red (12-11).

Note: Published 12 November 1957.   Collier Books in New York
   published a paperback (No. AS345X) edition of this title
   in 1962 for which type was reset.   Excerpts from "The
   Fiction Writer and His Country" appear in *The Added
   Dimension* [B14]; collected in *Mystery and Manners* [A6].

B7   PRIZE STORIES   1957

Title: PRIZE STORIES | 1957 | THE O. HENRY AWARDS | Selected
   and Edited by PAUL ENGLE | Assisted by CONSTANCE URDANG |
   DOUBLEDAY & COMPANY, INC., GARDEN CITY, NEW YORK, 1957

Collation: 208 x 136 mm.   Pp. 312.

Contents: "Greenleaf," pp. 15-36.

Binding: Black cloth boards printed in white on the spine.
   Top and bottom edges trimmed, fore edges rough trimmed,
   top edges stained aqua-green (144).   White dust jacket
   designed by Margot Tomes, printed in black, light grey-
   blue (190), a darker grey-blue (185-186), and light
   pinkish red (26-29).

Note: Published 10 January 1957.   This story was first published in *The Kenyon Review* [C.1956.6] and was the first-
   prize winner in the O. Henry Awards of 1957.   It is re-
   printed in *The Best American Short Stories of 1957*
   (14 November 1957) and collected in *A Good Man Is Hard
   to Find* [A2], *Three* [A4], and *Complete Stories* [A7].

B8 THE BEST AMERICAN SHORT STORIES 1958

Title: THE | [*in red (11-13)*)] *Best* | AMERICAN | SHORT STORIES |
1958 | [*decorative rule*] | *and the Yearbook of the American
Short Story* | [*rule*] | *Edited by* | MARTHA FOLEY and DAVID
BURNETT | [*publisher's device*] | HOUGHTON MIFFLIN COMPANY ·
BOSTON | The Riverside Press Cambridge | 1958

Collation: 203 x 135 mm. Pp. xvi, 362.

Contents: "A View of the Woods," pp. 192-212.

Binding: Grey-yellow (near 90) cloth boards printed in dark
brown (59) on front and spine. All edges trimmed. White
dust jacket designed by Ivan Chermayeff printed in black,
yellowish pink (26), orange-yellow (67), and greenish
blue (172).

Note: Published 23 September 1958. A Ballantine paperback
edition of this book was published in March 1959. "A
View of the Woods" was first published in *The Partisan
Review* [C.1957.5]; reprinted in *Prize Stories of 1959* on
5 February 1959; collected in *Everything That Rises Must
Converge* [A5] and *Complete Stories* [A7].

B9 FICTION OF THE FIFTIES 1959

Title: Fiction of | the Fifties | A DECADE OF AMERICAN
WRITING | STORIES SELECTED AND WITH AN INTRODUCTION BY |
Herbert Gold | DOUBLEDAY & COMPANY, INC., GARDEN CITY,
NEW YORK, 1959

Collation: 208 x 138 mm. Pp. 383.

Contents: "A Word from Writer Directly to Reader," p. 26;
first publication. Reprints "The Artificial Nigger,"
pp. 284-304.

Binding: Grey (264-265) cloth boards, printed in purplish red
(255) on front and in purplish red and black on spine.
Top and bottom edges trimmed, outer edges rough trimmed.
White dust jacket designed by Alex Tsao printed in black,
purplish pink (247), and deep purplish red (256).

Note: Published 19 November 1959. Paperback edition published
as Dolphin Book No. C299 by Doubleday in 1961.

B10   40 BEST STORIES FROM MADEMOISELLE   1960

Title: [*on a double spread*] 40 *best stories* | EDITED BY |
    [*rule*] | *Harper & Brothers, Publishers* || *from Mademoiselle*
    1935-1960 | CYRILLY ABELS AND MARGARITA G. SMITH | [*rule*] |
    New York

Collation: 213 x 142 mm.   Pp. x, 479.

Contents: "The Capture," pp. 446-455.

Binding: Black cloth boards, printed in reddish purple (237)
    on front, silver and reddish purple on spine.   Top and
    bottom edges trimmed, fore edges rough trimmed.

Note: Published in March 1960.   Issued in black paper slip-
    case.   A paperback selection titled *Best Stories from
    Mademoiselle* was published by Popular Library (No. W1111),
    New York, in November 1961 and contains O'Connor's story.
    "The Capture" was first published in *Mademoiselle*
    [C.1948.1] and is collected in *Complete Stories* [A7] in
    a different version titled "The Turkey."

B11   A MEMOIR OF MARY ANN   1961

Title: A MEMOIR | OF | MARY ANN | BY | THE DOMINICAN NUNS |
    OF | OUR LADY OF PERPETUAL HELP HOME | ATLANTA, GEORGIA |
    Introduction by Flannery O'Connor | FARRAR, STRAUS AND
    CUDAHY | NEW YORK

Collation: 202 x 133 mm.   Pp. viii, 134.

Contents: "Introduction," pp. 3-21.   First publication.

Binding: Medium green (145-144) cloth boards printed in black
    on spine.   All edges trimmed.   White dust jacket designed
    by Ben Feder Associates and printed in black, yellow-
    green (119), and blue (178-177).

Note: Published on 24 November 1961; second printing in
    January 1962; English edition published by Burns & Oates,
    London, in [1961], with a Catholic Book Club edition
    issued in England in [1961]; Dell paperback (#5551)
    issued December 1962.   This introduction is collected
    in *Mystery and Manners* [A6].

B12   ÉCRIVAINS AMÉRICAINS D'AUJOURD'HUI   1964

Title: PRÉSENCES | *contemporaines* | *ÉCRIVAINS AMÉRICAINS*
   D'AUJOURD'HUI | PAR | PIERRE BRODIN | JAMES BALDWIN –
   SAUL BELLOW | TRUMAN CAPOTE – RALPH | ELLISON – JAMES
   JONES | NORMAN MAILER – BERNARD | MALAMUD – CARSON
   McCULLERS | ANAÏS NIN – FLANNERY | O'CONNOR – JAMES FARL |
   POWERS – PHILIP ROTH – JEROME | DAVID SALINGER – WILLIAM |
   STYPON – HARVEY SWADOS | JOHN UPDIKE | avec une chronologie
   des oeuvres | N. É. D., éditeur | 17, RUE DUGUAY –
   TROUIN – PARIS – 6ᵉ | 1964

Collation: 214 x 136 mm. Pp. 219 (plus a photograph of each
   writer).

Contents: Letter of 21 September 1963, pp. 206–207. Also
   contains a chapter on O'Connor, pp. 125–133.

Binding: White paper wrappers printed in black and red (11).
   Edges trimmed. White dust jacket printed in black, red-
   orange (34), orange (50–48), and orange-yellow (67).

Note: Published 5 September 1964.

B13   PRIZE STORIES   1965

Title: PRIZE STORIES 1965: | THE O. HENRY AWARDS | *Edited by*
   Richard Poirier and William Abrahams | WITH AN INTRODUCTION
   BY WILLIAM ABRAHAMS | DOUBLEDAY & COMPANY, INC., GARDEN
   CITY, NEW YORK | 1965

Collation: 209 x 137 mm. Pp. 295.

Contents: "Revelation," pp. 1–20; first book publication.

Binding: Yellow-green (130–131) cloth boards printed in black
   and gold on spine. Top and bottom edges trimmed, fore
   edges rough trimmed. White dust jacket designed by
   Robert Flynn printed in black, deep green (142–141),
   medium yellow (87–84), and greenish blue (169).

Note: Published 2 April 1965. "Revelation" was first pub-
   lished in *The Sewanee Review* [C.1964.4]; collected in
   Everything That Rises Must Converge [A5] and *Complete*
   Stories [A7]. This story was the first-prize winner in
   the O. Henry Awards in 1965, and marked the third time
   O'Connor was so honored.

B14   THE ADDED DIMENSION   1966

Title: THE ADDED DIMENSION | The art and mind | of Flannery
    O'Connor | [*device*] | *Edited by* | MELVIN J. FRIEDMAN *and*
    LEWIS A. LAWSON | *Fordham University Press : New York*

Collation: 228 x 151 mm.   Pp. 309.

Contents: Selection of letters to William Sessions, 1956-64,
    pp. 212-225 (first publication); A Collection of State-
    ments, pp. 226-260 (mainly first book publications);
    "Fiction Is a Subject with a History--It Should Be Taught
    That Way," pp. 264-268; "Some Aspects of the Grotesque in
    Southern Literature," pp. 270-279.

Binding: Brown-orange (51-54) cloth boards, printed in deep
    reddish brown (41) on spine. All edges trimmed. White
    dust jacket designed by J. Richard Palmer, printed in
    light brown (67) and medium brown (58).

Note: Published 15 November 1966.

B15   THE BOOKS IN FRED HAMPTON'S APARTMENT   1973

Title: RICHARD STERN | [*rule*] | The Books | in | Fred
    Hampton's | Apartment | E. P. DUTTON & CO., INC.
    [*vertical rule*] NEW YORK [*vertical rule*] 1973

Collation: 210 x 136 mm.   Pp. 303.

Contents: "Flannery O'Connor: A Remembrance and Some Letters,"
    pp. 209-216.   Slight changes were made after first publica-
    tion in *Shenandoah* [C.1965.1].

Binding: Medium red-brown (43-39) cloth boards, stamped in
    gold on spine. All edges trimmed. White dust jacket
    printed in black, deep violet (208), and brown-orange
    (54-57).

Note: Published 22 March 1973.

B16   THE BEST AMERICAN SHORT STORIES   1979

Title: The Best | AMERICAN | SHORT | STORIES | 1979 | [*rule*] |
    Selected from | U.S. and Canadian Magazines | by Joyce
    Carol Oates | with Shannon Ravenel | *With an Introduction*
    by Joyce Carol Oates | *Including the Yearbook of the* |
    American Short Story | [*publisher's device*] | 1979 |
    Houghton Mifflin Company Boston

Collation: 211 x 142 mm. Pp. xxii, 352.

Contents: "An Exile in the East," pp. 28-38.

Binding: Yellow (83-84) cloth boards printed in blue (178)
    and black on front cover and spine. All edges trimmed.

Note: Published 30 October 1979. This story was first pub-
    lished in *The South Carolina Review* [C.1978.1].

Section C
Contributions to Periodicals

Flannery O'Connor's first appearances in print came in publications issued at Georgia State College for Women. (For early published art work see Section E.) *The Corinthian* was the creative writing journal at GSCW to which O'Connor contributed throughout her college career (1942-45). Following college, the range of journals printing her written work reflects a rapid maturity with inclusion in such forums as *Accent*, *The Hudson Review*, *The Sewanee Review*, *The Kenyon Review*, and *Partisan Review* as well as periodicals with a more specialized circulation. Furthermore, there was a period when she reviewed books for *The Bulletin* and *The Southern Cross*, two Catholic laymen's newspapers in Georgia.

The first time a periodical is cited in this section, the city of its origin is given in parentheses. Within each year the numbering sequence is consecutive, beginning anew at the start of the year. Thus, "C.1948.2" cites "The Capture," the second periodical appearance in 1948.

1942

C.1942.1   "Going to the Dogs"
           The Corinthian (Milledgeville), 18, No. 2 (Fall),
           14.   [Article]

C.1942.2   [Review of *The Story of Ferdinand* by Munro Leaf]
           The Corinthian, 18, No. 2 (Winter), 14.

C.1942.3   "Why Worry the Horse?"
           The Corinthian, 18, No. 2 (Winter), 15.   [Essay]

1943

C.1943.1   "Elegance Is Its Own Reward"
           The Corinthian, 18, No. 2 (Spring), 7, 18.
           [Story]

C.1943.2   "Effervescence"
           The Corinthian, 18, No. 2 (Spring), 16.   [Verse]

C.1943.3   "Home of the Brave"
            The Corinthian (December), 5-7, 18.   [Story]

C.1943.4   "Doctors of Delinquency"
            The Corinthian (December), 13, 19.   [Essay]

                              1944

C.1944.1   "Biologic Endeavor"
            The Corinthian (Spring), 7, 18.   [Essay]

C.1944.2   [Unsigned, untitled note]
            The Corinthian (Fall), [3].   This note appears
            at the foot of the contents page and deals with
            characters in the O'Connor drawing on the cover.

C.1944.3   "Excuse Us While We Don't Apologize"
            The Corinthian (Fall), 4.   Signed "The Editor."
            [Editorial]

C.1944.4   "Fashion's Perfect Medium"
            The Corinthian (Fall), 12-13, 16.   Accompanied
            by O'Connor linoleum cuts.   [Essay]

C.1944.5   "Pftt"
            The Corinthian (Fall), 16.   [Verse]

                              1945

C.1945.1   [Untitled note]
            The Corinthian (Spring), [3].   Signed "Editor,"
            this note appears at the foot of the contents
            page and concerns the cover drawing probably
            done by O'Connor.

C.1945.2   "Notwithstanding"
            The Corinthian (Spring), 5.   Unsigned editor's
            note.

C.1945.3   "Higher Education"
            The Corinthian (Spring), 8.   [Verse]

C.1945.4   "Experiment Harmless"
            The Corinthian (Spring), 9.   Unsigned note pre-
            ceding class sketches of Dr. Taylor, Dean of
            Instruction.

C.1945.5   "Education's Only Hope"
           The Corinthian (Spring), 14-15.   [Essay]

1946

C.1946.1   "The Geranium"
           Accent (Urbana), 4, No. 4 (Summer), 245-253.
           Collected in *Complete Stories* [A7].

1948

C.1948.1   "The Train"
           The Sewanee Review (Sewanee), 56, No. 2 (April-
           June), 261-271. Revised and expanded as Chapter
           1 of *Wise Blood* [A1]; collected in *Complete
           Stories* [A7].

C.1948.2   "The Capture"
           Mademoiselle (New York), 28 (November), 148-149,
           195-196, 198-201. Reprinted in *40 Best Stories
           from Mademoiselle 1935-1960* [B10] and collected
           under its earlier title "The Turkey" in *Complete
           Stories* [A7].

1949

C.1949.1   "The Heart of the Park"
           Partisan Review (New York), 16, No. 2 (February),
           138-151. Revised as Chapter 5 of *Wise Blood* [A1];
           collected in *Complete Stories* [A7].

C.1949.2   "The Woman on the Stairs"
           Tomorrow (New York), 8, No. 12 (August), 40-44.
           Retitled "A Stroke of Good Fortune," this story
           appeared in *Shenandoah* (Lexington, Virginia), 4,
           No. 1 (Spring 1953), 7-18, and is the fourth
           story in *A Good Man Is Hard to Find* [A2]; collec-
           ted in *Complete Stories* [A7].

C.1949.3   "The Peeler"
           Partisan Review, 16, No. 12 (December), 1189-
           1206. Revised as Chapter 3 of *Wise Blood* [A1];
           collected in *Complete Stories* [A7].

1952

C.1952.1   "Enoch and the Gorilla"
           New World Writing, First Mentor Selection (New
           York), No. 1 (April), 67-74. This story appears
           rewritten as Chapter 11 of *Wise Blood* [A1]; col-
           lected in *Complete Stories* [A7].

1953

C.1953.1   "The Life You Save May Be Your Own"
           The Kenyon Review (Gambier, Ohio), 15, No. 2
           (Spring), 195-207. The first book appearance
           came in *Prize Stories 1954* [B4]; this is the
           third story in *A Good Man Is Hard to Find* [A2]
           and was reprinted in *Perspectives U.S.A.* #14
           (Winter 1956); collected in *Complete Stories*
           [A7].

C.1953.2   "The River"
           The Sewanee Review, 61, No. 3 (Summer), 455-475.
           This is the second story in *A Good Man Is Hard
           to Find* [A2]; collected in *Complete Stories* [A7].

C.1953.3   "A Late Encounter with the Enemy"
           Harper's Bazaar (New York), 87, No. 4 (September),
           234, 247, 249, 252. This is the eighth story in
           A Good Man Is Hard to Find [A2]; collected in *Com-
           plete Stories* [A7].

1954

C.1954.1   "A Circle in the Fire"
           The Kenyon Review, 16, No. 2 (Spring), 169-190.
           First book publication came in *Prize Stories 1955*
           [B4]; this is the seventh story in *A Good Man Is
           Hard to Find* [A2]; collected in *Complete Stories*
           [A7].

C.1954.2   "A Temple of the Holy Ghost"
           Harper's Bazaar, 88, No. 2910 (May), 108-109, 162-
           164, 169. [There is also a substantial quotation
           from one of O'Connor's letters in the "Editor's
           Guest Book," p. 54.] This is the fifth story in
           A Good Man Is Hard to Find [A2]; collected in
           Complete Stories [A7].

C.1954.3 "The Displaced Person"
      The Sewanee Review, 62, No. 4 (Autumn), 634-654.
      This is the tenth story in *A Good Man Is Hard to
      Find* [A2]; collected in *Complete Stories* [A7].

1955

C.1955.1 "The Artificial Nigger"
      The Kenyon Review, 17, No. 2 (Spring), 169-192.
      This is the sixth story in *A Good Man Is Hard to
      Find* [A2]; reprinted in *The Best American Short
      Stories of 1956* [B5] and *Fiction of the Fifties*
      [B9]; collected in *Complete Stories* [A7].

C.1955.2 "Good Country People"
      Harper's Bazaar, 89, No. 2923 (June), 64-65, 116-
      117, 121-122, 124, 130. This is the ninth story
      in *A Good Man Is Hard to Find* [A2]; reprinted in
      the *Cluster Review*, Seventh Issue (March 1965),
      9-12, 17-20; collected in *Complete Stories* [A7].

C.1955.3 "You Can't Be Any Poorer Than Dead"
      New World Writing, No. 8 (October), 81-97. This
      story appears rewritten as Chapter 1 of *The
      Violent Bear It Away* [A3]; collected in *Complete
      Stories* [A7].

1956

C.1956.1 [Review of *The Presence of Grace* by J.F. Powers]
      The Bulletin (Savannah), 31 March. Extracts in
      Mystery and Manners [A6].

C.1956.2 [Review of *The Malefactors* by Caroline Gordon]
      The Bulletin, 31 March.

C.1956.3 [Review of *Two Portraits of St. Therese of Lisieux*
      by Etienne Robo]
      The Bulletin, 26 May.

C.1956.4 [Review of *Humble Powers* (Three Novelettes) by Paul
      Horgan]
      The Bulletin, 6 June.

C.1956.5 [Review of *Letters from Baron Friedrich von Hügel
      to a Niece*, ed. Gwendolen Greene]
      The Bulletin, 23 June.

C.1956.6   "Greenleaf"
            The Kenyon Review, 18, No. 3 (Summer), 384-410.
            This is the second story in *Everything That Rises
            Must Converge* [A5]; reprinted in *Prize Stories
            1957* [B7]; collected in *Complete Stories* [A7].

C.1956.7   [Review of *Beyond the Dreams of Avarice* by Russell
            Kirk]
            The Bulletin, 21 July.

C.1956.8   [Review of *The Catholic Companion to the Bible* by
            Ralph L. Woods]
            The Bulletin, 1 September.

C.1956.9   [Review of *Meditations before Mass* by Romano Guar-
            dini]
            The Bulletin, 24 November.

                            1957

C.1957.1   [Review of *The Metamorphic Tradition in Modern
            Poetry* by Sister Bernetta Quinn]
            The Bulletin, 5 January.

C.1957.2   [Review of *Writings of Edith Stein* by Edith Stein]
            The Bulletin, 2 March.

C.1957.3   "The Church and the Fiction Writer"
            America (New York), 96 (30 March), 733-735.
            Excerpts in *The Added Dimension* [B14]; collected
            in *Mystery and Manners* [A6].

C.1957.4   [Review of *Criticism and Censorship* by Walter F.
            Kerr]
            The Bulletin, 11 May.

C.1957.5   "A View of the Woods"
            Partisan Review, 24, No. 4 (Fall), 475-496.
            First book publication came in *The Best American
            Short Stories of 1958* [B8]; this is the third
            story in *Everything That Rises Must Converge*
            [A5]; collected in *Complete Stories* [A7].

1958

C.1958.1   ["Motley Special: Interview with Flannery O'Connor,
           Correspondence to Questions by Students"]
           The Motley (Mobile, Alabama), 9, No. 1 (Spring),
           29-31. (Arranged by Frank O'Hara.) Excerpt in
           The Added Dimension [B14].

C.1958.2   [Review of *The Transgressor* by Julian Greene]
           The Bulletin, 3 May.

C.1958.3   [Review of *Patterns in Comparative Religion* by
           Mircea Eliade]
           The Bulletin, 12 July.

C.1958.4   "The Enduring Chill"
           Harper's Bazaar, 91, No. 2960 (July), 44-45,
           94, 96, 100-102, 108. This is the fourth story
           in *Everything That Rises Must Converge* [A5];
           collected in *Complete Stories* [A7].

C.1958.5   [Review of *American Classics Reconsidered* by H.C.
           Gardiner, S.J.]
           The Bulletin, 1 November.

C.1958.6   [Review of *Israel and Revelation* by Eric Voegelin]
           The Bulletin, 15 November.

C.1958.7   [Review of *Late Dawn* by Elizabeth Vandon]
           The Bulletin, 29 November.

1959

C.1959.1   [Review of *Freud and Religion* by Gregory Zilboorg]
           The Bulletin, 10 January.

C.1959.2   [Review of *Temporal and Eternal* by Charles Péguy]
           The Bulletin, 10 January.

C.1959.3   ["A Symposium on the Short Story"--Replies to Two
           Questions]
           Esprit (Scranton, Pennsylvania), 3, No. 1
           (Winter), 10.

C.1959.4   [Review of *Harry Vernon at Prep* by Frank Smith]
           The Bulletin, 7 March.

1960

C.1960.1   ["An Interview with Flannery O'Connor and Robert
           Penn Warren"]
           Vagabond (Nashville), 4 (February), 9-17. Ex-
           cerpt in *The Added Dimension* [B14].

C.1960.2   [Review of *The Phenomenon of Man* by Teilhard de
           Chardin and *Pierre Teilhard de Chardin* by Claude
           Tresmontant]
           The Bulletin, 20 February.

C.1960.3   "The Comforts of Home"
           The Kenyon Review, 22, No. 4 (Autumn), 523-554.
           This is the fifth story in *Everything That Rises
           Must Converge* [A5]; collected in *Complete Stories*
           [A7].

C.1960.4   [Review of *The Science of the Cross* by Edith Stein]
           The Bulletin, 1 October.

C.1960.5   [Review of *Beat on a Damask Drum* by T.K. Martin]
           The Bulletin, 1 October.

C.1960.6   [Review of *Pierre Teilhard de Chardin* by Nicolas
           Corte]
           The Bulletin, 15 October.

C.1960.7   [Review of *Soul and Psyche* by Victor White, O.P.]
           The Bulletin, 29 October.

C.1960.8   [Review of *Christian Initiation* by Louis Bouyer]
           The Bulletin, 12 November.

C.1960.9   [Review of *Modern Catholic Thinkers*, ed. A. Robert
           Capronegri]
           The Bulletin, 24 December.

1961

C.1961.1   "Symposium on the Teaching of Creative Writing"
           [statement]
           Four Quarters (Philadelphia), 10, No. 2 (January),
           20.

C.1961.2   ["Recent Southern Fiction: A Panel Discussion"]
           Bulletin of Wesleyan College (Macon), 41, No. 1

          (January), 3, 5, 10-15. Excerpt in *The Added
          Dimension* [B14].

C.1961.3   [Review of *The Divine Milieu* by Pierre Teilhard de
           Chardin]
           The Bulletin, 4 February.

C.1961.4   "The Partridge Festival"
           The Critic (Chicago), 19, No. 4 (February-March),
           20-23, 82-85. Collected in *Complete Stories* [A7].

C.1961.5   "The Novelist and Free Will"
           Fresco (Detroit), I, No. 2 (Winter), 100-101.
           (An editorial note mentions that this piece is
           made up of portions of two letters by O'Connor
           to Winifred McCarthy.) Reprinted in *The Added
           Dimension* [B14].

C.1961.6   [Review of *Catholics in Conversation* by Donald
           McDonald]
           The Bulletin, 4 March.

C.1961.7   [Review of *The Life of St. Catherine of Siena* by
           Raymond of Capua]
           The Bulletin, 18 March.

C.1961.8   [Review of *Cross Currents*, ed. Joseph E. Cunneen]
           The Bulletin, 1 April.

C.1961.9   "Mary Ann: The Story of a Little Girl"
           Jubilee (St. Paul), 9, No. 1 (May), 28, 30-32,
           35. (Table of contents mistakenly lists article
           as "Mary Jane.") First published in book form
           in *A Memoir of Mary Ann* [B11]; collected in
           Mystery and Manners [A6]. An excerpt titled
           "Mystery of Suffering" was published in *Catholic
           Mind*, 9 (Fall 1962), 23-29.

C.1961.10 "Everything That Rises Must Converge"
           New World Writing, No. 19, pp. 74-90. This is
           the first story in *Everything That Rises Must
           Converge* [A5]; collected in *Complete Stories* [A7].

C.1961.11 [Review of *The Conversion of Augustine* by Romano
           Guardini]
           The Bulletin, 10 June.

C.1961.12 [Review of *Stop Pushing* by Dan Herr]
           The Bulletin, 10 June.

C.1961.13   [Review of *The Critic*]
             The Bulletin, 10 June.

C.1961.14   [Review of *Life's Long Journey* by Kenneth Walker]
             The Bulletin, 24 June.

C.1961.15   [Review of *Selected Letters of Stephen Vincent
             Benet*, ed. Charles Fenton]
             The Bulletin, 5 August.

C.1961.16   "Living with a Peacock"
             Holiday (New York), 30, No. 3 (September), 52,
             110-112, 114. First published in book form in
             Mystery and Manners [A6] as "The King of the
             Birds."

C.1961.17   [Review of *Themes of the Bible* by J. Guillet, S.J.]
             The Bulletin, 16 September.

C.1961.18   [Review of *The Resurrection* by F.X. Durrwell,
             C.S.S.R.]
             The Bulletin, 16 September.

C.1961.19   [Review of *The Mediaeval Mystics of England*, ed.
             Eric Colledge]
             The Bulletin, 30 September.

C.1961.20   [Note on *The Phenomenon of Man*]
             American Scholar (Washington, D.C.), 30, No. 4
             (Autumn), 618.   (Written in response to an invita-
             tion for writers to identify the outstanding
             books of the past three decades.)

C.1961.21   [Review of *Freedom, Grace, and Destiny* by Romano
             Guardini]
             The Bulletin, 28 October.

C.1961.22   [Review of *The Range of Reason* by Jacques Maritain]
             The Bulletin, 25 November.

C.1961.23   [Review of *The Bible and the Ancient Near East*,
             ed. G.E. Wright, and *The Old Testament and Modern
             Study*, ed. H.H. Rowley]
             The Bulletin, 9 December.

C.1961.24   [Review of *The Novelist and the Passion Story* by
             F.W. Dillistone]
             The Bulletin, 23 December.

C.1961.25 [Review of *Teilhard de Chardin* by Oliver Rabut,
           O.P.]
           The Bulletin, 23 December.

                              1962

C.1962.1   [Review of *Conversations with Cassandra* by Sister
           M. Madeleva]
           The Bulletin, 6 January.

C.1962.2   [Review of *Talk Sense!* by Edward Gryst]
           The Bulletin, 3 February.

C.1962.3   [Review of *Christian Faith and Man's Religion* by
           Marc C. Ebersole and *Christianity Divided*, ed.
           Daniel J. Callahan, Heiko A. Oberman, and Daniel
           J. O'Hanlon]
           The Bulletin, 17 February.

C.1962.4   [Review of *Jubilee*, ed. Edward Rice]
           The Bulletin, 17 February.

C.1962.5   [Review of *Evidence of Satan in the Modern World*
           by Leon Christiani]
           The Bulletin, 2 March.

C.1962.6   [Review of *The Georgia Review*, quarterly, University
           of Georgia Press]
           The Bulletin, 2 March.

C.1962.7   [Review of *The Conscience of Israel* by Bruce Vawter,
           C.M.]
           The Bulletin, 17 March.

C.1962.8   [Review of *The Victorian Vision* by Margaret M.
           Maison]
           The Bulletin, 31 March.

C.1962.9   [Review of *Toward the Knowledge of God* by Claude
           Tresmontant]
           The Bulletin, 12 May.

C.1962.10 "The Lame Shall Enter First"
           The Sewanee Review, 70, No. 3 (Summer), 337-379.
           This is the sixth story in *Everything That Rises
           Must Converge* [A5]; collected in *Complete Stories*
           [A7].

C.1962.11   [Review of *The Cardinal Spellman Story* by Robert
             I. Gannon, S.J.]
             The Bulletin, 4 August.

C.1962.12   [Review of *The Council, Reform, and Reunion* by Hans
             Kung and *The Integrating Mind* by William F. Lynch,
             S.J.]
             The Bulletin, 4 August.

C.1962.13   [Review of *The Catholic in America* by Peter J.
             Rahill]
             The Bulletin, 24 November.

                                   1963

C.1963.1   [Review of *The Bible: Word of God in Words of Men*
             by Jean Levie]
             The Southern Cross (Savannah), 2 March.

C.1963.2   [Review of *Frontiers in American Catholicism* by
             Walter J. Ong, S.J.]
             The Southern Cross, 9 March.

C.1963.3   [Review of *New Men for New Times* by Beatrice
             Avalos and *Seeds of Hope in the Modern World*
             by Barry Ulanov]
             The Southern Cross, 16 March.

C.1963.4   "Fiction Is a Subject with a History--It Should
             Be Taught That Way"
             Georgia Bulletin (Atlanta), [Book Supplement]
             (21 March). Collected in *Mystery and Manners*
             [A6] as "Total Effect and the Eighth Grade."

C.1963.5   [Review of *The Wide World, My Parish* by Yves
             Congar, O.P.]
             The Southern Cross, 23 March.

C.1963.6   [Review of *Letters from a Traveler* by Pierre
             Teilhard de Chardin]
             The Southern Cross, 27 April.

C.1963.7   "Flannery O'Connor / An Interview"
             Jubilee, 11, No. 2 (June), 33-35. (Interview
             by C. Ross Mullins, Jr., photographs by Mullins.)
             Excerpts in *The Added Dimension* [B14] and *Mystery
             and Manners* [A6].

C.1963.8   "An Interview with Flannery O'Connor"
            The Critic, 21, No. 6 (June, July), 29-31.
            (Interviewed by Gerard E. Sherry.) Excerpt in
            The Added Dimension [B14].

C.1963.9   "Why Do the Heathen Rage?"
            Esquire (Chicago), 60, No. 1 (July), 60-61. Col-
            lected in *Complete Stories* [A7].

C.1963.10   [Review of *Saint Vincent De Paul* by M.V. Woodgate,
            The Holiness of Vincent De Paul by Jacques
            Delarue, and *St. Vincent De Paul* by Von Matt
            and Cognet]
            The Southern Cross, 11 July.

C.1963.11   [Review of *What Is the Bible?* by Henri Daniel-Rops
            and *Faith, Reason, and the Gospels*, ed. John J.
            Heaney, S.J.]
            The Southern Cross, 18 July. Reprinted in
            Catholic Week, 24 November.

C.1963.12   [Review of *Image of America* by Norman Foerster and
            The Modern God by Gustave Weigel, S.J.]
            The Southern Cross, 26 September.

C.1963.13   [Review of *Evangelical Theology: An Introduction*
            by Karl Barth]
            The Southern Cross, 24 October.

C.1963.14   [Review of *The Cardinal Stritch Story* by Maria
            Buehrle and *Leo XIII: A Light from Heaven* by
            Br. William Kiefer, S.M.]
            The Southern Cross, 31 October.

C.1963.15   "The Regional Writer"
            Esprit, 7, No. 1 (Winter), 2, 31-35. Excerpts
            in *The Added Dimension* [B14], collected in
            Mystery and Manners [A6].

C.1963.16   [Review of *Morte d'Urban* by J.F. Powers]
            The Southern Cross, 29 November.

1964

C.1964.1   [Review of *Prince of Democracy: James Cardinal
            Gibbons* by Arline Boucher and John Tehan]
            The Southern Cross, 9 January.

C.1964.2   [Review of *The Kingdom of God: A Short Bible*, ed.
           Louis J. Putz, C.S.C.]
           The Southern Cross, 9 January.

C.1964.3   ["Flannery O'Connor--A Tribute" (by numerous con-
           tributors)]
           Esprit, 8, No. 1 (Winter), 26-27.   [Contains long
           excerpts from O'Connor letters to Sr. Mariella
           Gable, O.S.B.]

C.1964.4   "Revelation"
           The Sewanee Review, 72, No. 2 (Spring), 178-202.
           This story was first published in book form in
           Prize Stories 1965 [B13], and is the seventh
           story in *Everything That Rises Must Converge*
           [A5]; collected in *Complete Stories* [A7].

C.1964.5   "The Role of the Catholic Novelist"
           Greyfriar (Loudonville, N.Y.), 7 (1964), 5-12.
           A much different version of this was printed as
           "Catholic Novelists and Their Readers" in
           Mystery and Manners [A6].   Excerpt in *The Added
           Dimension* [B14].

                              1965

C.1965.1   "Flannery O'Connor: A Remembrance and Some Letters"
           by Richard Stern
           Shenandoah, 16, No. 2 (Winter), 5-10.   Contains
           ten letters from O'Connor to Stern; reprinted
           with expanded comments by Stern in *The Books
           in Fred Hampton's Apartment* [B15].

C.1965.2   "Some Aspects of the Grotesque in Southern Litera-
           ture"
           Cluster Review (Macon, Georgia), Seventh Issue
           (March), 5-6, 22.   Reprinted in *Forthcoming*
           (Commerce, Texas), 10, No. 1 (1967), 9-12, in a
           rewritten form.   The *Cluster Review* version is
           close to that reprinted in *The Added Dimension*
           [B14] and in *Mystery and Manners* [A6].   There
           are a number of differences in some sentences
           between *The Added Dimension* and *Mystery and Man-
           ners* versions, with considerable differences in
           paragraphing.

C.1965.3   "Parker's Back"
           Esquire, 63, No. 4 (April), 76-78, 151-152, 154-

155. This is the eighth story in *Everything That Rises Must Converge* [A5]; collected in *Complete Stories* [A7].

C.1965.4 "My Mentor, Flannery O'Connor" by Sr. Mary-Alice, O.P.
Saturday Review (New York), (29 May 1965), 24-25. Contains long excerpts from O'Connor letters to Sr. Mary-Alice.

C.1965.5 "An Interview with Flannery O'Connor" by Katherine Fugina, Faye Rivard, and Margaret Sieh
Censer (Winona, Minnesota), (Summer), 53-56. Excerpt in *The Added Dimension* [B14].

1966

C.1966.1 "The Catholic Novelist in the Protestant South"
Viewpoint (Washington, D.C.), (Spring), 5-17. Collected in a different version in *Mystery and Manners* [A6].

1967

C.1967.1 ["Letter to Hugh Brown and English Club"]
Forthcoming (Commerce, Texas), 10, No. 1, 20.

C.1967.2 ["Letter to Paul W. Barrus"]
Forthcoming, 10, No. 1, 19.

1970

C.1970.1 "Wildcat"
The North American Review (Cedar Falls), 255, No. 1 (Spring), 66-68. Collected in *Complete Stories* [A7]. This issue also contains "Flannery O'Connor: A Reminiscence and Some Letters" by Jean Wylder, pp. 58-65.

C.1970.2 "The Barber"
The Atlantic (Boston), 226, No. 4 (October), 111-118. Collected in *Complete Stories* [A7].

1971

C.1971.1   "The Crop"
           Mademoiselle, 72, No. 6 (April), 216-217, 273-275.
           Collected in *Complete Stories* [A7].

1976

C.1976.1   "Lettres de Flannery O'Connor à M.E. Coindreau"
           Delta (Montpellier, France), No. 2 (March), 15-22;
           notes, 23-25. This entire issue of *Delta* is
           devoted to Flannery O'Connor and is subtitled
           "Flannery O'Connor et le réalisme des lointains."

C.1976.2   "Flannery, 1957" by Maryat Lee
           The Flannery O'Connor Bulletin (Milledgeville),
           V (Autumn), 39-60. Contains nine O'Connor letters
           with deletions; also contains excerpts from two
           other O'Connor letters.

1978

C.1978.1   "Exile in the East"
           The South Carolina Review (Columbia), II, No. 1
           (November), 12-21.

1979

C.1979.1   "A Master Class: From the Correspondence of
           Caroline Gordon and Flannery O'Connor," by Sally
           Fitzgerald
           The Georgia Review (Athens), XXXIII, No. 4
           (Winter), 827-846. Contains fragments of
           letters by O'Connor not included in *The Habit of
           Being*.

Section D
Miscellaneous Appearances in Print

D1 [Dust jacket blurb] *The End of Pity and Other Stories* by
    Robie Macauley. New York: McDowell, Obolensky, Inc.,
    1957.

D2 [Dust jacket blurb] *The Lime Twig* by John Hawkes. New
    York: New Directions, 1961.

D3 [Dust jacket blurb] *The Favourite--A Novel of the Court
    of Louis XIII* by Françoise Mallet-Toris. New York:
    Farrar, Straus & Cudahy, [1962].

D4 [Dust jacket blurb] *The Quiet Enemy* by Cecil Dawkins.
    New York: Atheneum, 1963.

D5 [Dust jacket blurb] *Teeth, Dying and Other Matters* by
    Richard Stern. New York: Harper & Row, 1964.

D6 [Broadside poem] "Higher Education," printed on one side
    of a single sheet, signed "Mary Flannery O'Connor" and
    issued in 1980 by the Palaemon Press in North Carolina
    in an edition of 126 copies (100 numbered, 26 lettered;
    both identical in format). This poem first appeared in
    The Corinthian in Spring 1945 [C.1945.3].

Section E
Early Published Art Work

E.I. *PEABODY PALLADIUM*

The Peabody School was maintained by Georgia State College for Women (now Georgia College) as a laboratory school for grades 1 through 12. It was being phased out in 1974 when only grades 1-3 were taught. Flannery O'Connor attended four years of high school at Peabody between 1938 and 1942, contributing linoleum block prints to the school newspaper, the *Peabody Palladium*. While no complete back file of this newspaper is preserved at the College or the Milledgeville Public Library, two copies (one of which is damaged) may be found in the Flannery O'Connor Collection at Georgia College. References to her cartoons in the *Palladium* may be found in a clipping from that newspaper dated 16 December 1941 and another from the *Macon Telegraph and News* dated 13 June 1943, both in the O'Connor Collection.

E.I.1   "One Result of the New Peabody Orchestra" [lino-cut of girl playing saxophone, another with hands over her ears]. Vol. 4, No. 1 (28 October 1940), 2. (Mary Flannery O'Connor is listed as Art Editor on the masthead.)

E.I.2   "Bedlam?..." [lino-cut, damaged, only part of a figure with arms and legs askew]. Vol. 5, No. 4 (17 February 1942), 2. (O'Connor listed as Art Editor on masthead.)

E.II. *THE COLONNADE*

The Colonnade is the newspaper published by Georgia State College for Women (now Georgia College). Flannery O'Connor began contributing linoleum block illustrations to the paper early in her freshman year, in 1942, and these appeared in nearly every issue until she graduated in 1945. In the issue of 6 March 1943 the masthead was enlarged, and O'Connor's name was added for the first time as Art Editor. Except for school holidays and the summer months, *The Colonnade* appeared weekly during O'Connor's freshman year, but on 28 September

1943 a bi-monthly publication schedule was announced. The
less frequent publication was caused by paper shortages and
decreased enrollment resulting from World War II.

O'Connor signed her linoleum blocks in two ways: with a
construction of her initials "M.F.O'C.," which formed a little
bird, or with a "C" within an "O" (similar to the copyright
symbol). For each of the signed items in the following
account, indication is given of the method of signing.

E.II.1   "The Immediate Results of Physical Fitness Day"
          [girl leaning on table while holding a walking-stick;
          signed with bird.] Vol. 17, No. 3 (9 October 1942), 4.

E.II.2   "Why Don't We Do This More Often?" [girl eating sand-
          wich; signed with bird]. Vol. 17, No. 4 (17 October
          1942), 4.

E.II.3   "Aw, nuts! I thought we'd have at least one day off
          after the faculty played softball." [two girls walking;
          signed with bird]. Vol. 17, No. 5 (24 October 1942),
          4.

E.II.4   "Oh gosh! I didn't know you had to pay a poll tax."
          [girl at ballot box, monitor standing nearby; signed
          with bird]. Vol. 17, No. 7 (7 November 1942), 4.

E.II.5   "Doggone this Golden Slipper Contest. Now we have to
          wear saddle oxfords." [two girls, one seated, one
          standing; signed with bird]. Vol. 17, No. 8 (14 Novem-
          ber 1942), 4.

E.II.6   "Term papers add quite a lot to these Thanksgiving
          holidays." [girl with suitcase, umbrella, and books;
          signed with bird]. Vol. 17, No. 9 (21 November 1942),
          4.

E.II.7   "Are you glad to be back?" [two girls at library
          shelves; signed with bird]. Vol. 17, No. 10 (5 Decem-
          ber 1942), 4.

E.II.8   "In the light of our common knowledge, don't you con-
          sider this examination business rather superfluous?"
          [two girls walking; signed with bird]. Vol. 17, No.
          11 (12 December 1942), 4.

E.II.9   "Business as Usual" [crowd at door of bookstore,
          signed ©]. Vol. 17, No. 12 (2 January 1943), 4.

"Aw, nuts! I thought we'd have at least one day off after the faculty played softball!"

Linoleum block cartoon by O'Connor for *The Colonnade* (E.II.3)

"D you think teachers are necessary?"

Linoleum block cartoon by O'Connor for *The Colonnade* (E.II.28)

E.II.10   "Aw, don't worry about not getting on the Dean's
          List.   It's no fun going to the picture show at
          night anyway." [two girls walking; signed with bird].
          Vol. 17, No. 13 (9 January 1943), 4.

E.II.11   "I don't enjoy looking at these old pictures either,
          but it doesn't hurt my reputation for people to think
          I'm a lover of fine arts." [two girls standing in
          front of a painting; signed ©]. Vol. 17, No. 14
          (16 January 1943), 4.

E.II.12   "Officer or no officer, I'm going to ask her to let
          me try on that hat." [two girls waiting for 2 WAVEs
          to come by on sidewalk; signed with bird]. Vol. 17,
          No. 15 (23 January 1943), 4.

E.II.13   "But I tell you, you don't have to get a rooster to
          tell you when to get up; all you have to do is set
          your clock back." [two girls talking; signed with
          bird]. Vol. 17, No. 16 (30 January 1943), 4.

E.II.14   "Now why waste all your energy getting physically
          fit?   You'll never look like a WAVE anyhow." [two
          girls watching a third exercise; signed with bird].
          Vol. 17, No. 17 (6 February 1943), 4.

E.II.15   "Traffic" [girl looking down from tree where she
          escaped a platoon of WAVEs marching on sidewalk;
          signed ©]. Vol. 17, No. 18 (13 February 1943), 4.

E.II.16   "See there, I told you they didn't keep gunpowder in
          those things." [two girls watching WAVE open her
          purse; signed with bird]. Vol. 17, No. 19 (20 Febru-
          ary 1943), 4.

E.II.17   "It's a shame nobody petitioned me for an office.   I
          could have done much more for Faculty-Student rela-
          tions." [two girls talking; signed with bird]. Vol.
          17, No. 20 (27 February 1943), 4.

E.II.18   "Oh, give me back my raincoat; you still look more
          like a moron than a WAVE." [girl looking at a photo-
          graph as WAVE overhears her comment; signed with
          bird]. Vol. 17, No. 21 (6 March 1943), 4.

E.II.19   "Coming back affects some people worse than others."
          [girl standing on head reading while two others walk
          by, signed with bird]. Vol. 17, No. 22 (20 March
          1943), 2.

E.II.20   "Targets are where you find 'em!" [girl with bow and
          arrow, target to right, platoon of WAVEs marching
          away to left; signed with bird]. Vol. 18, No. 23
          (27 March 1943), 2.

E.II.21   "Oh, well, I can always be a Ph.D." [girl wearing
          glasses sitting on side lines at student dance;
          signed with bird]. Vol. 18, No. 24 (3 April 1943),
          2.

E.II.22   "If we moved all those hats on the wrong hooks, do
          you think we'd still be eligible for the Dean's
          List?" [two girls looking at a row of WAVEs' hats
          and coats on numbered hooks; signed with bird]. Vol.
          18, No. 24 (3 April 1943), 2.

E.II.23   "I think it's perfectly idiotic for the Navy not to
          let you WAVES dress sensibly like us college girls."
          [two girls talking to a pair of WAVEs; signed with
          bird]. Vol. 18, No. 25 (10 April 1943), 2.

E.II.24   "Wake me up in time to clap!" [girl speaking to her
          friend at back of auditorium during a lecture;
          signed ©]. Vol. 18, No. 26 (17 April 1943), 2.

E.II.25   "Aw quit trying to tell me that thing means she's
          a MESSENGER. I'm not as dumb." [two girls watching
          WAVE walk by with armband reading MESS; signed with
          bird]. Vol. 18, No. 27 (15 May 1943), 2.

E.II.26   "Those are the kind of WAVES I like." [five girls
          watching two sailors walk by; signed with bird].
          Vol. 18, No. 28 (22 May 1943), 2.

E.II.27   "Gosh, we're glad to be back" [four girls looking
          dejected; signed with bird]. Vol. 19, No. 1 (28 Sep-
          tember 1943), 2.

E.II.28   "Do you think teachers are necessary?" [girl with
          large stack of books talking to friend; signed with
          bird]. Vol. 19, No. 2 (5 October 1943), 2.

E.II.29   "They give us entirely too much work. I can't
          manage but six outside activities!" [two girls under
          an umbrella; signed with bird]. Vol. 19, No. 3
          (19 October 1943), 2.

"They give us entirely too much work. I can't manage but six outside activities!"

Linoleum block cartoon by O'Connor for *The Colonnade*
(E.II.29)

"*I understand it's a form of physic maladjustment created by a marked dissatisfaction with a change in environment wherein the family unit is disrupted—called homesickness.*"

Linoleum block cartoon by O'Connor for *The Colonnade* (E.II.44)

E.II.30   "Could I interest you in buying a Contemporary
          Georgia syllabus?" [student offering booklet to
          WAVE; signed with bird]. Vol. 19, No. 4 (9 November
          1943), 2.

E.II.31   "Just the thought of getting away from here for a
          few days unhinges some people, you know." [two girls
          watch another girl leading a turkey on a string;
          signed with bird]. Vol. 19, No. 5 (23 November 1943),
          2.

E.II.32   "I wonder if there could be anything to that business
          about studying at the first of the quarter?" [two
          girls studying at table beneath light bulb, clock at
          3:00 a.m.; signed with bird]. Vol. 19, No. 6
          (14 December 1943), 2.

E.II.33   "I hear there's a shortage of classrooms." [eight
          figures holding class on a rooftop; unsigned].
          Vol. 19, No. 7 (4 January 1944), 2.

E.II.34   "This can never be done in ten minutes." [students
          with umbrellas walking through rain on way to classes;
          signed with bird]. Vol. 19, No. 8 (18 January 1944),
          2.

E.II.35   "Two mo' monts we won't be a-doin' it...." [four
          Negroes and dog in foreground as platoon of WAVEs
          marches away in background; signed with bird].
          Vol. 19, No. 9 (1 February 1944), 2.

E.II.36   "Kilpatrick was fair." [two girls standing outside
          building; reference is to chapel lecture on 8 Feb-
          ruary 1944 by Dr. W.H. Kilpatrick, noted Georgia
          educator; signed with bird]. Vol. 19, No. 10
          (15 February 1944), 2.

E.II.37   "I believe the totalitarian outlook of the aggressive
          minority in the educational-governmental faction
          should be crushed, and if I am elected sixth vice
          recording secretary, I shall bend every effort to
          crush it." [girl at lectern delivering campaign
          speech; signed with bird]. Vol. 19, No. 11 (29 Feb-
          ruary 1944), 2.

E.II.38   "I hope the rules of that place slacken up before we
          start going out with girls." [two boys in short pants
          walking by front gate to GSCW; signed with bird].
          Vol. 19, No. 12 (7 March 1944), 2.

E.II.39   "Madam Chairman, the committee has reached a decision."
           [several girls in heap on floor, one girl standing
           with black eye; signed with bird]. Vol. 19, No. 13
           (4 April 1944), 2.

E.II.40   "Counter-Attack" [several WAVEs climbing up tree
           with arrows stuck in their backsides, girl with bow
           and arrow on ground; this is the tallest lino cut
           in any issue of *The Colonnade*, running the height of
           the page. Others are between 4 inches and 7 inches
           while this is nearly 15 inches; signed with bird].
           Vol. 19, No. 14 (18 April 1944), 2.

E.II.41   "The whole family's been wintering here at GSCW--you
           have to take what you can get these days." [group of
           dogs lounging near fireplug and shrubbery; signed
           with bird]. Vol. 19, No. 15 (2 May 1944), 2.

E.II.42   "This place will never amount to anything until they
           get a Student Committee on Faculty Relations." [two
           disgruntled students sitting on steps, one with shoes
           off; signed with bird]. Vol. 19, No. 17 (23 May
           1944), 2.

E.II.43   "It breaks my heart to leave for a whole summer."
           [girl jumping into air as four others watch; signed
           with bird]. Vol. 19, No. 18 (30 May 1944), 2.

E.II.44   "I understand it's a form of physic [sic] maladjust-
           ment created by a marked dissatisfaction with a change
           in environment wherein the family unit is disrupted--
           called homesickness." [two girls observing another
           with crossed eyes clutching her side and throat;
           signed with bird]. Vol. 20, No. 1 (26 September
           1944), 2.

E.II.45   "Now if 50,000 paratyphoid bacillae can go through
           the eye of a needle abreast, that ought to put at
           least 500,000,000,000 in that spoonful; and you
           should be ill by early tomorrow morning." [girl
           talking to another at dinner table; signed with bird].
           Vol. 20, No. 2 (10 October 1944), 2.

E.II.46   "Understand, I got nothing against getting educated,
           but it just looks like there ought to be an easier
           way to do it." [two girls standing with books beneath
           umbrella; signed with bird]. Vol. 20, No. 3 (24 Oc-
           tober 1944), 2.

E.II.47   "I demand an honorary organization for the C-Group!"
           [girl standing before the Dean's desk; signed with
           bird]. Vol. 20, No. 4 (18 November 1944), 2.

E.II.48   "... and I ask you--how many Pilgrim Fathers had to
           write term-papers during Thanksgiving." [girl
           jumping on books as another watches; signed with
           bird]. Vol. 20, No. 5 (6 December 1944), 4.

E.II.49   "Do you have any books the faculty doesn't particu-
           larly recommend?" [girl asking question of another
           at library circulation desk; signed with bird].
           Vol. 20, No. 6 (24 January 1945), 4.

E.II.50   "I understand she says it's the happy way of doing
           things." [two girls at blackboard watching another
           enter class in a formal dress with corsage; signed
           with bird]. Vol. 20, No. 7 (7 February 1945), 4.

E.II.51   [Untitled] [girl running up walk behind a formation
           of WAVEs, bumping them on the legs with an umbrella
           as she goes by; signed with bird]. Vol. 20, No. 8
           (22 February 1945), 4.

E.II.52   [Untitled] [three girls looking at a pair of feet
           sticking out of a mudhole; signed with bird]. Vol.
           20, No. 9 (7 March 1945), 4.

E.II.53   "She says we're on the threshold of social revolu-
           tion." [mother talking to father while daughter
           shows them an open book; signed with bird]. Vol. 20,
           No. 10 (5 April 1945), 4.

E.II.54   "Hrump--Not enough pride to build a nest." [nesting
           eagle speaking to two babies as airplane flies over
           dropping bombs; signed with bird]. Vol. 20, No. 11
           (19 April 1945), 4.

E.II.55   "Isn't it fortunate that Genevieve has completely
           escaped that boy-crazy stage?" [girl's eyes pop out
           of her head as she walks by two boys with her mother
           and friend; signed with bird]. Vol. 20, No. 12
           (2 May 1945), 4.

E.II.56   "You don't mind if I get comfortable, do you?"
           [dentist with drill in hand sitting in lap of patient
           with open mouth; signed with bird]. Vol. 20, No. 13
           (22 May 1945), 4.

E.II.57   "Yeah, I know it's a nice shoe, lady, but it's not
          exactly what I'm looking for." [sailor speaking to
          saleslady as he tries on a black and white wingtip;
          signed with bird]. Vol. 20, No. 14 (6 June 1945), 4.

E.III. *THE ALUMNAE JOURNAL OF THE
GEORGIA STATE COLLEGE FOR WOMEN*

Mainly, the *Alumnae Journal* selected cartoons by O'Connor
which had already appeared in *The Colonnade*; however, the
first two which she contributed to the *Journal* had not been
published elsewhere.

E.III.1   [Untitled] [girl in graduation cap and gown; signed
          ©]. Vol. 8, No. 1 (Winter 1942), 3.

E.III.2   [Untitled] [WAVE in uniform; signed ©]. Vol. 8, No.
          1 (Winter 1942), 3. Note on p. 17 credits these
          first two lino-cuts to O'Connor.

E.III.3   "Traffic." Vol. 8, No. 2 (Spring 1943), 15. Reprint
          of E.II.15.

E.III.4   "Aw, nuts! I thought we'd have at least one day
          off...." Vol. 9, No. 3 (Spring 1944), 4. Reprint
          of E.II.3. Note on p. 2 credits O'Connor for the
          block prints in the Spring 1944 issue.

E.III.5   "Just the thought of getting away...." Vol. 9, No. 3
          (Spring 1944), 8. Reprint of E.II.31.

E.III.6   "Do you think teachers are necessary?" Vol. 9, No. 3
          (Spring 1944), 9. Reprint of E.II.28.

E.III.7   "I wonder if there could be anything to that business
          about studying...." Vol. 9, No. 3 (Spring 1944), 19.
          Reprint of E.II.32.

E.III.8   "They give us entirely too much work...." Vol. 9,
          No. 3 (Spring 1944), 21. Reprint of E.II.29.

E.III.9   "Understand, I got nothing against getting educa-
          ted...." Vol. 10, No. 1 (Winter 1944), 14. Reprint
          of E.II.46.

E.III.10   "I understand it's a form of physic [sic]...."
           Vol. 10, No. 1 (Winter 1944), 21.   Reprint of
           E.II.44.

E.III.11   [Untitled].   Vol. 10, No. 3 (Spring 1945), 13.
           Reprint of E.II.51.

E.IV. *THE CORINTHIAN*

    The creative writing journal at Georgia State College
for Women, *The Corinthian*, published written contributions
from Flannery O'Connor from the beginning of her freshman
year, 1942-43, through the close of her senior year, 1944-45.
As a senior, O'Connor served as Editor of *The Corinthian*.
It was during her year as Editor that O'Connor's characteris-
tic cartoons and illustrations were published in the GSCW
creative writing journal.

E.IV.1   [Untitled cover illustration] [four girls with um-
         brella standing in a puddle, one kneeling, all scowling
         at the border which forms the name and issue of the
         journal; unsigned].   (Fall 1944), cover.

E.IV.2   [Untitled] [girl with back to mirror; unsigned].
         (Fall 1944), 12.   This and the next three illustra-
         tions accompany O'Connor's article, "Fashion's Perfect
         Medium" [C.1944.4].

E.IV.3   [Untitled] [girl with umbrella; unsigned].   (Fall
         1944), 12.

E.IV.4   [Untitled] [girl with back to mirror, different from
         E.IV.2; unsigned].   (Fall 1944), 13.

E.IV.5   [Untitled] [girl wearing long string of beads, un-
         signed].   (Fall 1944), 13.

E.IV.6   [Untitled] [girl with pointed foot and pointed finger;
         signed *Q*].   (Fall 1944), 14.   This and the next three
         illustrations accompany the article "You Can Have My
         Share" by Joyce Moncrief.

E.IV.7   [Untitled] [girl with book leaning against post;
         signed *Q*].   (Fall 1944), 14.

E.IV.8   [Untitled] [girl seated in modern dance position;
           signed Q]. (Fall 1944), 15.

E.IV.9   [Untitled] [girl reading while walking; signed Q].
           (Fall 1944), 15.

E.IV.10   [Untitled cover illustration] [fat, booted figure in
           Sam Brown belt and large hat lounging at table beneath
           an umbrella; unsigned]. (Spring 1945), cover.

                        E.V. *THE SPECTRUM*

   Since Flannery O'Connor completed work on her B.A. in three
years, the yearbooks for 1943, 1944, and 1945 are the only ones
reflecting her college activities. Her cartoons formed a significant part of the yearbooks for 1944 and 1945, and during
her senior year she held the post of Feature Editor for *The
Spectrum*. Thus, the 1945 annual is organized by features for
which O'Connor cartoons form headpieces that help set the mood.

E.V.1   [Untitled] [girl blowing out a candle; unsigned].
           (1944), 74. While most of the linoleum cuts in *The
           Spectrum* for 1944 are unsigned, Flannery O'Connor is
           credited for them on p. 90 in a note on the yearbook
           staff.

E.V.2   [Untitled] [girl with large gavel; unsigned]. (1944),
           74.

E.V.3   [Untitled] [large girl with tennis racquet; unsigned].
           (1944), 74.

E.V.4   [Untitled] [girl with open book in left hand; unsigned].
           (1944), 88.

E.V.5   [Untitled] [girl scratching head; unsigned]. (1944),
           88.

E.V.6   [Untitled] [girl reading long newspaper; unsigned].
           (1944), 88.

E.V.7   [Untitled] [group of seven students seated on sofa and
           chairs; unsigned]. (1944), 96.

E.V.8   [Untitled] [girl reading in bed; unsigned]. (1944),
           127.

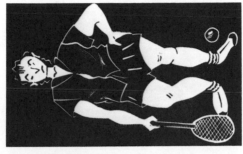

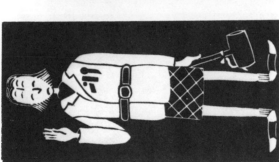

Untitled linoleum block cartoons by O'Connor for the 1944 *Spectrum* (E.V.1, E.V.2, E.V.3)

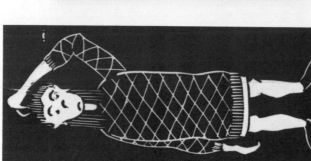

Untitled linoleum block cartoons by O'Connor for the 1944 *Spectrum*
(E.V.4, E.V.5, E.V.6)

Untitled linoleum block cartoon by O'Connor for the 1944 *Spectrum*
(E.V.7)

Untitled linoleum block cartoon by O'Connor for the 1944 *Spectrum* (E.V.8)

E.V.9   [Untitled] [large scene with WAVE troops marching on
           sidewalk in rain, students attempting to avoid water-
           filled holes, and several dogs; signed MFO'Connor].
           (1945); this two-page illustration forms the front and
           back endpapers for the 1945 yearbook.

E.V.10   "This is Jessieville." [facade of columned building,
           two sleeping dogs in front; unsigned]. (1945), [4].
           Enlarged for p. 8. This is the first of a series of
           nine drawings, each devoted to a phase of life at
           GSCW chosen to be featured in the yearbook. "Jessie-
           ville" was the nickname of GSCW, and the continuity
           of the 1945 annual was envisioned as "A Pilgrimage
           through Jessieville" (the heading for facing pages
           4-5 containing nine O'Connor drawings which are later
           enlarged as section heads).

E.V.11   "They Guide Us on Our Way" [back view of a tall, thin
           and a short, fat faculty member, both in cap and gown;
           unsigned]. (1945), [4]. Enlarged for p. 16.

E.V.12   "Wayfarers" [four girls, one in front holding high
           stack of books; unsigned]. (1945), [4]. Enlarged
           for p. 28.

E.V.13   "Our Naval Escort" [short student reaching up toward
           a WAVE; unsigned]. (1945), 5. Enlarged for p. 78.

E.V.14   "We Learn to Lead" [one girl with gavel, one with
           candle, one with golf club; unsigned]. (1945), 5.
           Enlarged for p. 82.

E.V.15   "We Record Our Travels" [one girl kneeling and
           writing, two others sitting on her back reading papers;
           unsigned]. (1945), 5. Enlarged for p. 96.

E.V.16   "Points of Interest" [group: one girl standing on her
           head, one playing a violin, one lecturing, one kneeling
           to look through a magnifying glass; unsigned]. (1945),
           5. Enlarged for p. 104.

E.V.17   "Having a Wonderful Time" [girl and sailor dancing
           while two seated chaperons look on; unsigned]. (1945),
           5. Enlarged for p. 134.

E.V.18   "Where Our Pennies Go" [two girls walking, large one
           drinking a soda while small one carries sacks of gro-
           ceries; unsigned]. (1945), 5. Enlarged for p. 146.

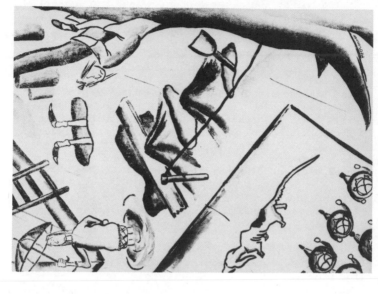

Endpapers by O'Connor for the 1945 *Spectrum* (E.V.9)

Section F
Translations of O'Connor's Works

Czech

F1 "Soudný Den" and "Zjevení" in *Světová Literatura*, 12,
No. 3 (1967), 44-56, 57-69. Translation by Frantisek
Vrba of "Judgement Day" and "Revelation."

Dutch

F2 "De Hoed" in *Moderne Amerikaanse Verhalen*. Edited by
Dola de Jong. Amsterdam: Polak and van Gennep, 1966,
pp. 331-350. Translation of "Everything That Rises
Must Converge."

F3 *De Kreupelen Zullen Ons Voorgaan*. Utrecht/Antwerp: A.W.
Bruna & Son, 1969. Pp. 131. Translation by Else Hoog
of "The Lame Shall Enter First," "Judgement Day," "Everything That Rises Must Converge," and "A View of the Woods."
(Paperback)

French

F4 *La Sagesse dans le sang*. Paris: Gallimard, 1959. Pp.
228. A translation with preface by Maurice-Edgar Coindreau
of *Wise Blood*. Regular trade edition plus 35 numbered
copies and 6 *hors commerce* lettered A-F. (Paperback)

F5 *Les Braves Gens ne courent pas les rues*. Paris: Gallimard,
1963. Pp. 233. A translation by Henri Morisset of *A Good
Man Is Hard to Find*. Regular trade edition plus 26 numbered copies. (Paperback)

F6 *Et ce sont les violents qui l'emportent*. Paris: Gallimard,
1965. Pp. 247. A translation by Maurice-Edgar Coindreau
of *The Violent Bear It Away*, with a preface by J.M.G.
LeClézio. Regular trade edition plus 27 numbered copies.
(Paperback)

F7   "Le Jour de jugement" in *La Nouvelle Revue Française*
      (October 1966), pp. 626-647. Translation by Henri
      Morisset of "Judgement Day."

F8   "La Fête des azalées" in *La Nouvelle Revue Française*
      (October 1968), pp. 399-428. Translation by Michel
      Gresset and Claude Richard of "The Partridge Festival."

F9   *Mon Mal vient de plus loin.* Paris: Gallimard, 1969. Pp.
      271. Translation by Henri Morisset of *Everything That
      Rises Must Converge.* Regular trade edition plus 26
      numbered copies. (Paperback)

F10   "A la mémoire de Mary Ann" in *La Nouvelle Revue Française*
      (December 1970), pp. 48-60. Translation by André Simon
      of the introduction to *A Memoir of Mary Ann.*

F11   *Pourquoi ces nations en tumulte?* Paris: Gallimard, 1975.
      Pp. 170. Translation by Claude Fleurdorge, Michel
      Gresset, and Claude Richard of "The Geranium," "The
      Barber," "The Wildcat," "The Crop," "The Turkey," "The
      Partridge Festival," and "Why Do the Heathen Rage?"
      (Paperback)

F12   *Le Mystère et les moeurs.* Paris: Gallimard, 1975. Pp.
      246. Translation by André Simon of *Mystery and Manners.*
      (Paperback)

                                German

F13   *Ein Kreis im Feuer.* Hamburg: Claasen Verlag, 1961.
      Pp. 252. Translation by Elisabeth Schnack of *A Good
      Man Is Hard to Find.* Contains eight of the original
      ten stories with "A Stroke of Good Fortune" and "A Temple
      of the Holy Ghost" omitted. (Boards)

F14   *Das brennende Wort.* Munich: Carl Hanser Verlag, 1962.
      Pp. 199. Translation by Leonore Germann of *The Violent
      Bear It Away.* (Boards and paperback)

F15   "Überhebe ja sich Keiner" in *Exkursionen*, ed. Leonore
      Germann. Munich: Carl Hanser Verlag, 1964, pp. 283-299.
      Translation by Leonore Germann of "Everything That Rises
      Must Converge."

F16   *Ein Kreis im Feuer.* Hamburg: Rowohlt, 1967. Pp. 157.
      Translation by Elisabeth Schnack of *A Good Man Is Hard*

to *Find*.   Contains the same eight stories as F13.   (Paperback)

F17 "Ein letztes Treffen mit dem Feind" in *Moderne amerikan-
ische Prosa*.   Berlin: Verlag Volk und Welt, 1967, pp.
291-307.   Translation by Elisabeth Schnack of "A Late
Encounter with the Enemy."

F18 *Ein Herz aus Feuer*.   Cologne: Benziger Verlag, 1972.
Pp. 276. Translation by Leonore Germann of *The Violent
Bear It Away*.   (Boards)

Greek

F19 *Kai I Viastai Arpazousi Aftin*....   Athens: G. Fexis,
1965.   Pp. 158.   Translation by Alexander Kotzias of *The
Violent Bear It Away*.   (Paperback)

Hungarian

F20 *Minden Összefut*.   Budapest: Európa Könyvkiadó, [1968].
Pp. 266.   Translation by Geher István, László Balázs,
B. Nagy László, and Osztovits Levente of *Everything
That Rises Must Converge*.   (Paperback)

Italian

F21 *Prospetti*.   Rome: Casa Editrice Sansoni, 1956.   Contains
translation of "The Life You Save May Be Your Own."
[Not seen]

F22 *Il cielo e dei violenti*.   Torino: Einaudi, 1965.   Pp.
221.   Translation by Ida Omboni of *The Violent Bear It
Away*.   (Boards)

F23 *La vita che salvi può essere la tua*.   Torino: Einaudi,
1968.   Pp. 399.   Translation by Ida Omboni of *A Good Man
Is Hard to Find* and *Everything That Rises Must Converge*.
(Boards)

Japanese

F24 *Hageshiku Semura Kore O Ubau*.   Tokyo: Shinchosha, 1971.
Pp. 203.   Translation by Saeki Schoichi of *The Violent
Bear It Away*.   [Not seen]

F25   *Taiyaku O'Connor*. Tokyo: Nan'Un-Do Co., Ltd., [1977].
      Pp. 125. Translation of "A Good Man Is Hard to Find"
      and "Greenleaf" published in a bilingual edition. (Paper-
      back with dust jacket)

                              Norwegian

F26   *Dommens Dag*. Oslo: Gyldendal, 1971. Pp. 290. Transla-
      tion by Aase Kagge of *A Good Man Is Hard to Find*. [Not
      seen]

                               Polish

F27   *26 Wspolczesnych Opowiadan Amerykanskich*. Warsaw: Iskry,
      1963. Pp. 552. Contains translation by Jan Dehnel of
      "Good Country People."

F28   *Trudno o Dobrego Cziowieka*. Warsaw: Państwowy Instytut
      Wydawniczy, 1970. Pp. 301. Translation by Maria Skib-
      niewska of "Everything That Rises Must Converge," "A View
      of the Woods," "The Enduring Chill," "The Lame Shall
      Enter First," "Revelation," "The River," "The Life You
      Save May Be Your Own," "A Temple of the Holy Ghost,"
      "The Artificial Nigger," "A Late Encounter with the
      Enemy," "Good Country People," and "A Good Man Is Hard
      to Find." (Boards)

                               Spanish

F29   *Sangre sabia*. Barcelona: Molino, 1966. Pp. 224. Trans-
      lation by Armando J. Durán of *Wise Blood*.

F30   *Sangre sabia*. Barcelona: Editorial Lumen, 1966. Pp.
      224. Translation by Armando J. Durán of *Wise Blood*.
      (Paperback)

F31   *Las dulzuras del hogar*. Barcelona: Editorial Lumen,
      1968. Pp. 281. Translation by Vida Ozores of *Everything
      That Rises Must Converge*. (Paperback)

F32   *Un Hombre bueno no es facil de encontrar*. Barcelona:
      Editorial Lumen, 1973. Pp. 272. Translation by Marcelo
      Covián of *A Good Man Is Hard to Find*.

Swedish

F33   En *God Mand er Svaer at Finde.* Copenhagen: Grafisk
      Forlag, 1965. Pp. 222. Translation by Karina Windfeld-
      Hansen of *A Good Man Is Hard to Find.* (Paperback)

F34   "Hyggliga Människor Hittar Man Sällan," in *Modern
      Amerikansk Berättarkonst.* Stockholm: Bokforlaget
      Aldus/Bonniers, 1965, pp. 157-172. Translation by Lars
      Bjurman of "A Good Man Is Hard to Find." (Paperback)

F35   Och *Stormen For oss Vidare.* Stockholm: Gebers, 1967.
      Pp. 263. Translation by Carl Sundell of *The Violent
      Bear It Away.* (Paperback)

Section G
Film and Television Adaptations; Parodies

G1 "Galley Proof," a 23-minute WRCA-TV (NBC) film with
Harvey Breit interviewing Flannery O'Connor along with a
dramatization of "The Life You Save May Be Your Own."
Produced by Ann Keeley, directed by James Elson, with
technical direction by Gary Iorio. Tom T. Shiftlet
played by Sandy Kenyon; Mrs. Crater played by Mary Perry;
Lucynell played by Mildred Cook. [May 1955].

G2 "Playhouse of Stars," a CBS-TV film adaptation of "The
Life You Save May Be Your Own" with Gene Kelly, Agnes
Moorehead, and Janice Rule. Broadcast 1 March 1957.

G3 "The Life You Save May Be Your Own," typed screen adaptation by Gino Ardito, 15 pp. Copy in O'Connor Collection
at Georgia College. Dated 8 September 1963.

G4 "Directions 65" (Volume 5, No. 30), a 28-minute ABC-TV
show subtitled "A Tribute to Flannery O'Connor." Written
by Richard Gilman, produced by Wiley Hance, directed by
Robert De Laney. Interview by C. Ross Mullins [C.1963.7]
provides part of script for a portrayal of O'Connor
talking about writing. Scenes from *Wise Blood*, *The
Violent Bear It Away*, "The River," "The Displaced Person,"
and "A Good Man Is Hard to Find" are dramatized. Roles
played by Charles Durning, Larry Robinson, Carol Teitel,
and Eleanor Phelps. [1965].

G5 "The Displaced Person," a stage adaptation by Cecil
Dawkins. 87 pp. ditto typescript. Based on several
O'Connor stories. Directed by Edward Parone, this play
was produced at the American Place Theatre, New York,
opening on 29 December 1966.

G6 *Grim Fairy Tales for Adults* by Joel Wells. New York:
Macmillan, 1967. Contains a parody, "Winnie the Pooh by
Fl*nn*ry *'C*nn*r," pp. 117-122.

G7 "The World of Flannery O'Connor," produced and directed
by Jim Spitler. Narrated by Walter Sullivan. A documen-
tary film produced under the auspices of WDCN-TV and the
Nashville Public Television Council. 1974.

G8   "The Comforts of Home," produced by Leonard Lipson for
      Sholip Productions. A 40-minute film directed by Jerome
      Shore produced in 1973. It won a first prize in the
      1973 Atlanta Film Festival and was broadcast by PBS in
      1975.

G9   "Good Country People," adapted and directed by Jeff
      Jackson. A 32-minute film. 1975.

G10   "A Circle in the Fire," produced and directed by Victor
      Nunez. A 50-minute color film distributed by Perspective
      Films in Chicago. Shown over WNET in New York and
      public television stations in Houston and Miami as well
      as over the Cox Cable System. 1976.

G11   "The Displaced Person," produced by Matthew N. Herman,
      directed by Glenn Jordan, with Irene Worth as Mrs.
      McIntyre and John Houseman as Father Flynn. This film,
      part of the American Short Story series, was telecast
      by the Public Broadcasting System in April 1977. It is
      a one-hour segment in the series produced by Learning
      In Focus, Inc., Robert Geller, Executive Producer. In
      conjunction with the series, in 1977 Dell published the
      paperback *The American Short Story*, ed. Calvin Skaggs,
      which contains "The Displaced Person" and a discussion
      of this film as well as the others in the series.

G12   "Wise Blood." A feature film directed by John Huston,
      produced by Michael and Kathy Fitzgerald, with a screen-
      play by Benedict Fitzgerald. The cast includes Brad
      Dourif as Hazel Motes, Amy Wright as Sabbath Lily Hawks,
      Harry Dean Stanton as Asa Hawks, Dan Shor as Enoch Emory,
      Ned Beatty as Hoover Shoates, and Mary Nell Santacroce as
      the landlady. The picture opened commercially in the
      United States on 3 February 1980.

INDEX

Accent, C.1946.1
The Added Dimension, B14
Alther, Lisa, A2.I.c.1
America, C.1957.3
American Scholar, C.1961.20
American Signatures (see *New Signatures I*)
The Atlantic, C.1970.2
Avon Book of Modern Writing, B2

Balázs, László, F20
Baldwin, James, A4.I.a.1; B12
Barrus, Paul W., C.1967.2
Bellow, Saul, B12
The Best American Short Stories
  --1956, B5
  --1958, B8
  --1979, B16
Bjurman, Lars, F34
Book and Dust Jacket Designers
  Barss, William, B5
  Ben Feder Associates, B11
  Chermayeff, Ivan, B8
  Fleming, Guy, A6.T.a.1
  Flynn, Robert, B13
  Glaser, Milton, A1.I.a.2; A3.I.a.1
  Halmerson, A2.I.a.1
  Halverson, Janet, A8.I.a.1
  Johnson, Herb, A7.I.a.1
  Krupat, Cynthia, A8.I.a.1
  Manso, Leo, B6
  Nicholls, Guy, A1.I.b.1
  Palmer, J. Richard, B14
  Skaggs, Charles, A7.I.a.1
  Tomes, Margot, B3; B4; B7
  Tsao, Alex, B9

Book Clubs
  Catholic Book Club, B11
  Literary Guild Book Club, A5.I.a.1
  Saturday Review Book Club, A7.I.a.1
  Thomas More Book Club, A5.I.a.1; A7.I.a.1
Breit, Harvey, G1
Brodin, Pierre, B12
The Bulletin, C.1956.1; C.1956.2; C.1956.3; C.1956.4; C.1956.5;
    C.1956.7; C.1956.8; C.1956.9; C.1957.1; C.1957.2;
    C.1957.4; C.1958.2; C.1958.3; C.1958.5; C.1958.6;
    C.1958.7; C.1959.1; C.1959.2; C.1959.4; C.1960.2;
    C.1960.4; C.1960.5; C.1960.6; C.1960.7; C.1960.8;
    C.1960.9; C.1961.3; C.1961.6; C.1961.7; C.1961.8;
    C.1961.11; C.1961.12; C.1961.13; C.1961.14; C.1961.15;
    C.1961.17; C.1961.18; C.1961.19; C.1961.21; C.1961.22;
    C.1961.23; C.1961.24; C.1961.25; C.1962.1; C.1962.2;
    C.1962.3; C.1962.4; C.1962.5; C.1962.6; C.1962.7;
    C.1962.8; C.1962.9; C.1962.11; C.1962.12; C.1962.13
Bulletin of Wesleyan College, C.1961.2

Capote, Truman, A1.III.a.1; A4.I.a.1; B12
Catholic Mind, C.1961.9
Catholic Week, C.1963.11
Censer, C.1965.5
Clark, Eleanor, B2
Cluster Review, C.1955.2; C.1965.2
Coindreau, M.E., C.1976.1; F4; F6
Colette, B2
The Corinthian, C.1942.1; C.1942.2; C.1942.3; C.1943.1;
    C.1943.2; C.1943.3; C.1943.4; C.1944.1; C.1944.2;
    C.1944.3; C.1944.4; C.1944.5; C.1945.1; C.1945.2;
    C.1945.3; C.1945.4; C.1945.5
Covián, Marcelo, F32
The Critic, C.1961.4; C.1963.8

Dawkins, Cecil, G5; *The Quiet Enemy*, D4
Dehnel, Jan, F27
Delta, C.1976.1
Durán, Armando J., F29; F30

Ecrivains Américains d'Aujourd'hui, B12
Ellison, Ralph, B12
Esprit, C.1959.3; C.1963.15; C.1964.3
Esquire, C.1963.9; C.1965.3

Fiction of the Fifties, B9
Fitzgerald, Michael and Kathy, G12
Fitzgerald, Robert: "Introduction," A5.I.a.1; A5.II.a.1

Fitzgerald, Sally: "Introduction," A8.I.a.1
Fitzgerald, Sally and Robert, A6.I.a.1; A6.I.b.1
The Flannery O'Connor Bulletin, C.1976.2
Fleurdorge, Claude, F11
Forthcoming, C.1965.2; C.1967.1; C.1967.2

Geller, Robert, G11
Georgia Bulletin, C.1963.4
The Georgia Review, C.1962.6; C.1979.1
Germann, Leonore, F14; F15; F18
Giroux, Robert: "Introduction," A7.I.a.1
Gordon, Caroline, A1.I.a.1; *The Malefactors*, C.1956.2
Grau, Shirley Ann: *The Hard Blue Sky*, A4.I.a.1
Gresset, Michel, F8; F11
Greyfriar, C.1964.5

Harper's Bazaar, C.1953.3; C.1954.2; C.1955.2; C.1958.4
Hawkes, John: *The Lime Twig*, D2
Herman, Matthew N., G11
Holiday, C.1961.16
Hoog, Else, F3
Howe, Irving, B2
Hunter, Jim, A5.I.b.1
Huston, John, G12

Ionesco, Eugene, A5.I.b.1
István, Geher, F20

Jacket and Cover Blurbs
  Davidson, Donald, A1.I.a.2
  Gordon, Caroline, A1.I.a.1; A1.I.a.2; A3.I.a.1
  Goyen, William, A1.I.a.2; A2.I.a.1; A4.I.a.1
  Hicks, Granville, A1.I.a.2; A3.I.a.1; A3.II.a.1
  King, Francis, A5.II.a.1
  Levine, Paul, A1.I.a.2
  Prescott, Orville, A3.I.a.1; A3.II.a.1; A4.I.a.1
  Pritchett, V.S., A1.I.b.2
  Schott, Webster, A5.II.a.1
  Smith, Lillian, A5.II.a.1
  Solotaroff, Theodore, A5.II.a.1
  Waugh, Evelyn, A1.I.a.2; A1.I.b.1
Jackson, Jeff, G9
Jones, James, B12
Jubilee, C.1961.9; C.1962.4; C.1963.7

Kagge, Aase, F26
The Kenyon Review, C.1953.1; C.1954.1; C.1955.1; C.1956.6;
    C.1960.3

O'Connor, Flannery (cont'd)
    "Introduction" to *A Memoir of Mary Ann*, A6; B11 (see also
        "Mary Ann: The Story of a Little Girl")
    "Judgement Day," A5; A7
    "The King of the Birds," A6 (see also "Living with a
        Peacock")
    "The Lame Shall Enter First," A5; A7; C.1962.10
    "A Late Encounter with the Enemy," A2; A4; A7; C.1953.3
    "The Life You Save May Be Your Own," A2; A4; A7; B3;
        C.1953.1
    "Living with a Peacock," C.1961.16
    "Mary Ann: The Story of a Little Girl," C.1961.9
    Mystery and Manners, A6
    "Mystery of Suffering" (see "Mary Ann: The Story of a
        Little Girl")
    "The Nature and Aim of Fiction," A6
    Note on *The Phenomenon of Man*, C.1961.20
    "Notwithstanding," C.1945.2
    "Novelist and Believer," A6
    "The Novelist and Free Will," C.1961.5 (see also "On Her
        Own Work: In the Devil's Territory")
    "On Her Own Work: A Reasonable Use of the Unreasonable,"
        A6
    "On Her Own Work: In the Devil's Territory," A6 (see also
        "The Novelist and Free Will")
    "On Her Own Work: The Mystery of Freedom," A6
    "Parker's Back," A5; A7; C.1965.3
    "The Partridge Festival," A7; C.1961.4
    "The Peeler," A1.I.a.1; A7; C.1949.3
    "Pfft," C.1944.5
    "The Regional Writer," A6; C.1963.15
    "Revelation," A5; A7; B13; C.1964.4
    "Review of *The Presence of Grace* by J.F. Powers," A6;
        C.1956.1
    "The River," A2; A4; A7; C.1953.2
    "The Role of the Catholic Novelist," A6; C.1964.5
    "Some Aspects of the Grotesque in Southern Literature," B14;
        C.1965.2; "... in Southern Fiction," A6
    "A Stroke of Good Fortune," A2; A4; A7 (see also "The
        Woman on the Stairs")
    "The Teaching of Literature," A6
    "A Temple of the Holy Ghost," A2; A4; A7; C.1954.2
    Three by Flannery O'Connor, A4
    "Total Effect and the Eighth Grade" (see "Fiction Is a
        Subject with a History--It Should Be Taught That Way")
    "The Train," A1.I.a.1; A7; C.1948.1
    "The Turkey," A7
    Unsigned, untitled note, C.1944.2